D1557052

The Diwan Revisited

Discovered in the 1850s by the German explorer H. Barth, the *Diwan*, or genealogy, is a remarkable collection of facts, deeds, and descriptions of the sultans of Kanem-Bornu, one of the most advanced civilizations in West Africa. The *Diwan* has traditionally been perceived as a mere fragment of a larger set of the now-lost Royal achives, a compilation of biographies assembled by palace bureaucrats over the centuries. In *The Diwan Revisited*, Augustin Holl challenges such assumptions. Reevaluating almost 150 years of research, Holl agrees that the Diwan was most probably a segment of a larger, more diversified domain of literary genres– an epic originally situated within a thriving oral tradition.

Combining the latest advances in paleoclimatology, archaeology, social anthropology, ethnohistory, and linguistics, *The Diwan Revisited* is an ambitious, interdisciplinary endeavor.
It will add significantly to a deeper understanding of this fascinating historical document and to the early history and culture of West Africa in general.

Augustin F. C. Holl is a professor at the Department of Anthropology University of California, San Diego.

The Diwan Revisited
Literacy, State Formation and the Rise of Kanuri Domination (AD 1200-1600)

Augustin F.C. Holl

KEGAN PAUL INTERNATIONAL
London and New York

First published in 2000 by
Kegan Paul International Limited
UK: P.O. Box 256, London WC1B 3SW, England
Tel: 020 7580 5511 Fax: 020 7436 0899
E-mail: books@ keganpau.demon.co.uk
Internet: http://www.demon.co/uk/keganpaul/
USA: 562 West 113th Street, New York, NY 10025
Tel: (212) 666 1000 Fax: (212) 316 3100

Distributed by
John Wiley & Sons
Southern Cross Trading Estate
1 Oldlands Way, Bognor Regis
West Sussex, PO22 9SA, England
Tel: (01243) 779 777 Fax: (01243) 843 302
E-mail: cusservices@wiley.co.uk

Columbia University Press
61 West 62nd Street
New York, NY 10023, USA
Tel: (212) 459 0600
Internet: www.columbia.edu/cu/cup

Printed in Great Britain by IBT Global, London

ISBN 0-7103-0581-8

British Library Cataloguing in Publication Data
Holl, Augustin
The Diwan revisited: literacy, state formation and the rise of Kanuri domination
(AD 1200-1600) 1. Chad – History 2. Chad – Antiquities 1. Title. 967.4'3'01
ISBN 0710305818

Library of Congress Cataloging-in-Publication Data
Holl, Augustin
The Diwan revisited: literacy, state formation and the rise of Kanuri domination
(AD 1200-1600) / Augustin F.C. Holl
Includes bibliographical references. ISBN 0-7103-0581-8 1. Kanem-Bornu Empire--
Politics and government--Historiography. 2. Ibn Furtu, Ahmad fl. 1576-1578.
Diwan salatin Burnu. 3. Kanuri (African people)--Politics and government--
Historiography. I. Title. DT515.9B6H65 966.'801--dc21 97-23854 CIP

Contents

The Diwan Revisited

Preface

A living civilization is a drama of struggle between interpretations, outside influences, and emphases, an unrelenting struggle over what is the wheat and what is the chaff; rebellion for the sake of innovation, dismantling for the purpose of reassembling differently, and even putting things in storage to clear the stage for experiment and new creativity. And it is permissible to seek inspiration from and be fertilized by other civilizations as well. This implies a realization that struggle and pluralism are not just an eclipse or a temporary abberation but, rather, the natural climate for a living culture. (Amos Oz 1993: 137-8).

The research presented in this book has resulted from multiple attempts to integrate our archaeological work conducted in the Cameroonian part of the Chad plain into a wider pan-regional framework of social evolution. Historical events from Kanem, Bornu, Barguirmi and Wadday, to name but some of the major social formations of the Chad basin in the eighteenth and nineteenth centuries, have certainly been influential in shaping the evolutionary trajectories of the Kotoko polities and social systems. In this regard, the study of the emergence of centralized socio-political organization among the mound-dwellers of the Chadian plain could not be divorced from the understanding of the wider pan-regional sphere of social interaction between competing polities. In the past as well as in the present and for different reasons, people were moving from one area to another, social identities were shifting, being dissolved and reconstructed according to the vagaries of the balance of power between neighbouring communities, be they ethnic, occupational, and/or a combination of both, differentially integrated to produce some peculiar time- and place-specific traditions. In order to have access to a more profound understanding of such a dynamic process, it has appeared important to devise a new approach able to bring to light the inside or local view of the historical process which led to the formation, consolidation and expansion of the now famous

Kanem-Bornu empire or kingdom (s), the predominant state(s) formation in the Central Sudan for almost a millennium, from the ninth/tenth century AD to the end of the nineteenth century (Cuoq 1984, Fisher 1977, Lange 1985, 1990, Smith 1976, Urvoy 1949, Zeltner 1980, 1988). The Kanem-Bornu empire or kingdom(s) developed in the Chad basin, between the Borkou in the east, the Tibesti and the Fezzan in the north,, the Aïr in the west, the Hawsaland in the southwest, the Adamawa and Kotoko lands in the south, and finally, the Bhar el Ghazzal in the southeast. Political boundaries generally shifted, depending on the vagaries of alliances and warfare. They are in fact unknown for the larger part of early Kanem-Bornu history, and only slightly better known from the fifteenth-sixteenth century onwards. It is therefore not possible to give a straightforward and accurate picture of Kanem-Bornu territorial extent, from its obscur beginnings to its end.

The territorial extent, state bureaucracy, miltary and political organisation of the weakened 19th century Bornu kingdom are relatively well known for students of Central Sudan history (Barth 1965, Brenner 1973, Denham *et al.* 1826, Nachtigal 1980, Zeltner 1988). As far as territorial extent is concerned, it is almost coextensive with the present-day distribution of Kanuri speakers, with the Nigerian Bornu state as its core area, surrounded by conquered, annexed, and tributary territories in Niger, Nigeria Cameroon and Chad Republic. Birni Ghazzargamo, the capital city of the kingdom from the fifteenth century onwards, suffered from several Fulani attacks at the beginning of the nineteenth century. The kingdom was saved from total collapse by a coalition of Kanembu and Shuwa Arabs led by an intrepid warrior and scholar, Mohammed el Kanemi. With his followers, he founded a new settlement at Kukawa, further east, not far from the shore of lake Chad. Even if he was not yet explicitly ruling the country, his fame as learned man, adviser and war leader, resulted in the concentration of geniune political power in his hands for several years from 1808 to 1811, with the Sayfawa sultans transformed into puppet-kings. In 1812, he finally seized power and initiated the new Al Kanemi dynasty (Zeltner 1980: 200-1). In a kind of 'spoil-system', the new dynasty bureaucracy was filled with new Kanembu and Shuwa Arab officials, provoking long-term resentment from the now destituted former Kanuri elite. There were several attempts to overthrow the new rulers, but they all failed, ending in excecution of the conspirators. At the end of the nineteenth century, and more precisely in 1893, the weakened Bornu kingdom was an easy prey for the warrior-merchant Rabbeh. Kukawa was conquered and a new capital city was founded at Dikoa, approximately 100 km further south. Initiated in a context of expanding

European colonization, the Rabbeh domination of Bornu did not last for very long. On 22 April 1901, Rabbeh was defeated by French troops at the battle of Kusseri; on 5 September 1901, a decree was signed by the French government enacting the creation of 'Territoire Militaire des Pays et Protectorats du Tchad', with Commander Destenave as its first official (Zeltner 1988: 220).

The early part of Kanem-Bornu history is far less clearange The origin and development of centralized state systems, as well as processes of consolidation and expansion are subject to interesting debates among scholars. They agree and disagree, with varying emphasis, on several issues which will be considered here. As far as chronology is concerned, the emergence of centralized political system at an early stage is considered to have occurred in the ninth-tenth century AD (Cuoq 1984: 234-8, Fisher 1977: 287, Lange 1990: 474-8, Smith 1976: 159, Zeltner 1980: 29-38), with the formation of a Berber-derived or Zaghawa ruling dynasty. The second issue concerns a sustained shift from nomadic to sedentary life style with the foundation of cities, mostly capital cities for the rulers and their followers. The third is based on the integration of the Central Sudan into long-distance trade networks, linking the northern African coast to the hinterland, via the Fezzan and Kawarange On ideological and religious grounds, two aspects are generally agreed upon; they concern the existence of divine kinship and the advent and expansion of Islam.

The above mentioned issues are elegantly summarized by Fisher (1977: 288) in following terms: 'we have thus four elements of the classical Sudanese state formation situation: the nomadic intruder, the divine king, long-distance trade, and Islam'. There is some disagreement on the ethnic affiliation of the earliest ruling dynasty. For Cuoq (1984), Fisher (1977), Zeltner (1980) and Lange (1990), the Banu Duku who are considered to have ruled over Kanem from the eighth/tenth to the eleventh century, belonged to a Berber-derived tribe or the Zaghawa ethnic group. Smith (1976: 164) rejects the Berber connection, by which some researchers:

accepted uncritically the simple hypothesis that this history is merely the story of the way in which a group of Hamitic (Berber) invaders from the Sahara imposed a statelike political structure on a number of politically segmented Negro peoples of the Central Sudan.

For Smith, even if he proceeded with due caution, 'the antiquity of this word as an ethnic title is unknown. It may be of quite recent origin' (1976: 158), all the history of Kanem-Bornu kingdom(s) is confined within the context of the formation of the Kanuri people, with the ethnic label pushed backward to the end of the first millennium AD, to include 'a group of Teda-Daza speaking tribes forming a unified group in Kanem...' (1976: 158-9), 'as no earlier name for them appears to have been preserved' (1976: 159). Such a 'twist' solves the research problem before framing any accurate questions. Depending on authors, the development and expansion of Kanem-Bornu kingdom(s) is divided into three or four major periods. The first (eighth/tenth to eleventh century) corresponds to the rise in power of the Zaghawa Dugu dynasty, which also witnessed the development of divine kingship, with secluded kings. The second (eleventh to fourteenh century) is marked by the conversion of Sultan Hummay to Islam. It is characterized by the conquest of the Fezzan, the intensification of long-distance trade and the foundation of a capital city at Djimi on the Bahr el Ghazzal . These two periods are assumed to correspond to the earlier development of the Kanem kingdom which was later superseded by the Bornu one. For Smith (1976: 168) both periods are

subsumed under the heading of First Kanuri Empire, with the development a fief-holding aristocracy, an extensive class of princes (*Maïna*), appointed village headmen (*Bulama*), and a secular and religious bureaucracy with *Wazir, Khàzin, Tàlib*, and *qadi*. The third period (fourteenth to fifteenth century) coincides with a long-lasting series of troubles, involving competition between kins, factional conflicts, civil as well as external warfare, ending with the exodus, the abandonment of Kanem, and the foundation of a new kingdom in Bornu, on the western shore of Lake Chad. And finally, the fourth period (fifteenth to nineteenth century), characterized by the foundation of a new capital city at Birni Ghazzargamo corresponds to a kind of renaissance, or in Smith's (1976: 176) terms, the Second Kanuri Empire.

If taken at face value, the social and political achievement of the Kanem-Bornu rulers is very impressive: a single dynasty ruling different kingdoms and peoples for a millennium.

This dynasty founded in the ninth or tenth century AD, continued, though with many vicissitudes, to rule the Kanuri people and their dependants for the best part of a millennium. Here we have a political achievement of some magnitude and it is important for us to examine the bonds which held the tribes of the Kanuri peoples together in loyalty to the Sefawa over this remarkably long period and in addition brought under its control over the centuries a considerable number of non-Kanuri peoples. (Smith 1976: 160)

This achievement is based, according to all the consulted works, on a combination of factors: first a nomad *ethos* based on the pride in the nomad origin of the rulers' ethnic group, the preservation of various aspects of nomad life, and the conquest of desert oasis-dwellers; second, a military superiority resulting from effective use of cavalry; third, the social and political prestige of centralized government institutions anchored to divine kingship, linked to intermarriage with allied groups, be they clans or whole tribes; fourth, the sedentarization of tribes and the foundation of permanent capital cities; fifth, the introduction of and conversion to Islam and the development of learning and 'universalist' religion; and finally, sixth, the onset and intensification of long-distance trade.

The irony in all these lively reconstructions of the Kanem-Bornu millennium-long political system is that they are all, without any exception, based heavily of the exegesis of a single historical document. The chronology is obtained 'by working backwards through the reign lengths of the *Mais* (sultan or king in Kanuri) given in the *girgam* (or *Diwan*)' (Smith 1976: 166, note 35). The chronological framework deduced from the Diwan is probably the weakest component of the narrative of Kanem-Bornu history, as will be shown later in this work. Many other aspects of the Diwan have been ignored, and even discarded as meaningless. The first part of the Diwan, from the reign of Sayf ben Dhi Yazan to Sultan Hawa, is generally ignored. It is considered to belong to a legendary background, but, nonetheless, is called upon selectively, for example to support the existence of a Duku dynasty (the third king). The Diwan deserves better than this selective use, geared to support what each scholar thinks to be the genuine pathway to statehood.

Considered from this perspective, the Diwan of Kanem-Bornu kings appears to be a very interesting and intriguing document, containing a constellation of different but nested kinds of highly relevant social messages. We had however to look for some sort of adequate starting points to make sense of the different kinds of messages and the meanings of the observed patterns and structures, insofar as it seems almost axiomatic that there are always gaps between things themselves and descriptions, patterns, and structures, whether they are scientific or not (Bateson and Bateson 1988: 164-5), this difficulty being more acute when we are concerned with social phenomena. First of all, and however fine the mesh of our description, there are always some smaller details which will escape. Second, the continuum of nature is constantly broken down into a discontinuum of 'variables' in the act of description or specification; there are , therefore, additional gaps between kinds of description, which are not necessarily present in the pattern, structure or thing described. And finally, there is yet again a similar discontinuity within the hierarchy of descriptive and even explanatory statements. Consequently, it is not claimed that we have found 'the adequate methodology' as it seems obvious that even with the must powerful research tools, 'we would quickly find ourselves in an infinite regress'. (Bateson and Bateson 1988: 165). Metaphorically, however, the research presented is conceived as 'Russian dolls', with 'quantum' jumps from one level of description and meaning to another, shifting from the genealogy of the documents, to the discussion of contexts of preformance, then to the internal analysis of the Diwan, the early history of the Central Sudan considered in a wider framework and finally Kanuri domination and literacy as they are connected to the rise of Bornu kingdom. Each of the five parts of the book can thus be considered as a macro-level containing several micro-levels, each of which is of crucial importance for the understanding of the new explanation offered here to make sense of the Diwan of Kanem-Bornu. Finally, the major aim of this work is to revive the discussions on the development state formations in Sudanic Africa with a due emphasis on the inside views of the historical processes.

Acknowledgements

As often occurs in any kind of research, this work is in some sense a collective undertaking. We wish to thank Mr Mahammat Ngarba, our collaborator on archaeological excavation at Houlouf from 1984 to 1991, who acted as interpreter during the evening recording of oral history from the Kotoko walled settlement of Houlouf and the Shuwa Arab village of Alaya. Parts of this research were presented as a winter colloquium lecture at the Department of Anthropology at the University of California at San Diego in February 1993, and at the symposium 'State, Land and Society in the History of Sudanic Africa' held at the Center for African Studies of the University of Illinois at Urbana-Champaign in April 1993. We wish to thank all the participants for their comments and criticisms which have been important for the clarification of some aspects of the discussion. Special thanks are due to our colleague and friend Dr Thomas E. Levy who invited us to give a lecture in the winter colloquium series of his department, to Professor Donald Crummey, for inviting us to participate in the 20th Annual Symposium of the Center for African Studies, thus providing the opportunity to meet numerous scholars of the history of Sudanic Africa, Professor David N. Freedman, who gave us a copy of a stimulating and unpublished work on kingly chronologies of the dynasty of David and the kingdom of Judah, Professor Michael E. Meeker, for his keen interest and discussion on our lecture at San Diego, Professor Norman Yoffee who has read and commented on earlier versions of this work, and my colleagues from the Department of Ethnology and Prehistory of the University of Paris X at Nanterre, Drs Jacques Galinier and Patrick Menget. It is however obvious that none of them may be held responsible for any possible error or misunderstanding in the interpretation of the historical data conducted in this research.

Introduction

The Diwan Revisited: Aims and Purposes

Since H. Barth's travels and discoveries in North and Central Africa in the 1850s, a series of local written historical records from the 'Kanem-Bornu' kingdoms have been collected and sent to Europe, and have played a fundamental role in the development of the historical scholarship concerning the past of that part of the African continent. One set of these written historical records, the Diwan-or the list of kings of the Sayfawa dynasty-has become famous among the students of the history of the Central Sudan, and is considered by some researchers to provide the longest chronological chart of the rulers uncovered to date in Black Africa. Historical research has thus been focused on the singled-minded attempt to extract 'genuine' historical 'facts' from that important document, leading to an unending spiral of interpretation of interpretations, comments on comments. I do not suggest that the important interpretive works made by various scholars are useless; on the contrary, it is considered that with the accumulation of new data from other fields of research such as archaeology, social anthropology, palaeoenvironmental research, research on oral history and comparative mythology, a shift toward a wider anthropologically oriented interpretation is needed. It appears that the accumulated pieces of historical research dominant in the Central Sudan historiography, are enlightening on some points but at the same time, due to the nature of the academic traditions of the various authors engaged in the debate-historical philology versus local and internal approach-some other points, which may, at least theoretically, be considered as highly relevant for the understanding and the explanation of the dynamics of the past Kanem and Bornu social systems, have been obscured and sometimes simply posited as minor inconsistencies, resulting from copyists' mistakes.

'To be sure, the social occasions which concerns us (as anthropologically oriented students of the past) - whether it be something as conspicuous and formal as marriage ceremony or a sacrifice to the ancestors, or as mundane as a conversation or a court case, or a joking situation - have their recurrent shape and unity of structure. But the elements of which they are composed are of diverse structural and cultural provenance, appear and reappear in diverse situations. (Fortes 1969: 96)

Consequently, the present volume aims to explore other and discarded social aspects of the Diwan in order to asses their importance for a deeper understanding of the dynamics of the actual Kanem and Bornu social systems. In this perspective, the predominant political nature of literacy in African past societies will be emphasized; it is basically within this political framework characterized by fluctuating balance of power and social interaction, with trends toward integration countered by opposite trends toward desintegration, all of them pertaining to the changing aspects of the process of 'state' formation, that some of the inconsistencies recorded in the Diwan, start to make sense. It is argued that in the Central Sudan, literacy and the control of 'historical' knowledge, did not belong to the bureaucratic process of 'neutral' accumulation of palaces' or rulers' archives, but were instrumental in the complex process of competition for power, prestige and claims for ultimate legitimacy in the development of a centralized socio-economic system in the Chad Basin from c. 1200 to 1600.

A Methodological Sketch

The development of modern historical scholarship as exemplified in the research tradition on the past societies of the Bilad es Sudan in general, and more specifically on the Central Sudan, is connected with Islamology and Orientalism. As such, this tradition is characterized by heavy reliance on textual evidence alone which is studied following an above all philological approach. The philological approach aims to retrieve the original or archetypal frame of historical documents which are therefore considered to have been corrupted by lengthy series of interpolation and/or copyists' mistakes (Le Coran 1970), Vernant 1974). In so doing, inconsistencies and contradictions discovered are relegated to the status of mere accidents in the chain of transmission of historical information. These problems are more acute in research areas without written records (Vansina 1990) or possessing only a handful of such evidence like the Kanem-Bornu area (Lange 1977, 1987, Levtzion and Hopkins 1981). The philological research tradition has produced important breakthroughs in the understanding of some important parts of the history of Central Sudan and has generated interesting debates on the chronology of past societies and their political histories; the scope of our understanding of the past gained within the limits of the above mentioned approach is, however, severely limited regarding the range of social phenomena of interest for students of African history today. It is accepted that written records concern only a minute part of the transformations of societies from the past, that other kinds of data are needed to achieve a deeper understanding of the historical issues at hand, that oral history and social anthropology can be useful in clarifying some research problems (Connerton 1989, Okpewho 1979, Vansina 1985).

In order to achieve a deeper understanding of the Diwan or kings lists of Kanem and Bornu, before considering the long-lasting and important chronological and political aspects of the history of the area, we need to ask some naive questions which may be helpful to devise a problem-oriented research strategy. Such naive questions may be framed as follows: (1) How were these documents collected? (2) What is the genuine nature of the collected documents and how were they produced? (3) What were the socio-political contexts for their production? These questions capture the fundamental issues which will be addressed in this work. Due to the increased amount of research carried out in different fields of srudy in the Chad basin during the last decades, we are in a better position to ask different kinds of questions in an attempt to integrate the Diwan into a wider socio-historical perspective. In this regard, our exploratory model will be based on three major related aspects which will be investigated relatively independently from each other: the linguistic or, more precisely, the literary aspects of the documents which may allow the discovery of a deeper coherence and organization of the document, and make sense of the apparent inconsistencies or chaos; the anthropological aspects, which concern patterns of social and political interaction between individuals, small and larger social units and their transformations; and, finally, the historical aspects, which are concerned with the temporal frame of human action in the past at different scales. These different aspects will not be treated in a linear fashion, all of them are integrated differentially in the discussion of each of the selected themes. The methodology adopted here is therefore contextual and structural. Instead of proceeding from isolated 'facts', be they phonemes, words, sentences, toponyms, ethnonyms, titles, etc., the document is considered in its totality as a complex internal system of nested levels of meanings. In this perpective, a deeper understanding of the Diwan may emerge from the discovery of patterned relations between different, complementary and contradictory systems of meanings at various structural levels. Sound, musicality, rhythm, epic, etc. are such important systems of meanings, as are the social and political messages which are thus transmitted.

Part One

The Document

Prologue

The New Version of the Diwan

Readers who are not familiar with Central Sudan history may wish to know more about the dynastic list or the Diwan of Kanem-Bornu before going through the subtleties of our discussions. In this regard, we will start with the integral text of the document translated after the work of Lange (1977). It is considered that such a procedure will be useful for the understanding of our conclusions.

Opening
   This is the story of the sultans of Bornu.
   To start with the story of Sultan Sayf b. Dhi Yazan.
   His mother was from the Mekka, daughter of the king of Baghdad.
   He belonged to the Banu Sakas - others say Banu Sakasak - and also to the Makhzum.
   He was Sayf,
   son of al-Sahh, son of al-Sahh, son of Lu'ayy,
   son of Lu'ayy, son of Lu'ayy, son of al-Hadjdj,
   son of Bahr, son of (Abu al-Hadjdj), son of Djam,
   son of Hamla, son of Hud, son of Amir,
   son of Wardiyya, son of Halina, son of Kays,
   son of Quraysh, son of Abd Allah, son of Umar,
   son of Sa'd, son of Ismail, son of Ibrahim,

2

son of the brother of Tarakh Arghu Azar, son of Tajur, son of Sharukh,
son of Arkuma, son of Amir 'Abir, son of Shalakh,
son of Arfakhshadh Makhshadh, son of Sam, son of Nuh,
son of Lamak, son of Matushalakh Matusalim, son of Khanukh,
son of Zayd, son of Mabrak, son of Mahlayil Malyil,
son of (Qaynan) Kinana, son of Yanish,
son of Shit, son of Adam.
To him, greetings and blessing.

1 At his time, Sayf was the Master of the World in its four directions.
   When his end arrived,
   He died at Shimi.
   His reign lasted for twenty years.

2 Then came Sultan Ibrahim, son of Sayf.
   His mother was Aisha, daughter of K.rangem.
   His reign lasted for sixteen years.

3 Then came Sultan Duku, son of Ibrahim.
   His mother was Ghafalu, daughter of H.ra of the tribe of Kay
   And he also lived.
   He died at Y.ri Arangef.sa.
   His reign lasted for two hundred and fifty years.

4 Then came Sultan Funa, son of Duku
   He had been according to God's will.
   He died at M.lan in Kanem land.
   His reign lasted for sixty years.

5 Then came Arsu, son of Funa.
   His mother was Fukalshi.
   His reign lasted for fifty years.

6 Then came Sultan Katur, son of Arsu.

3

He also was the Master of the World.

He died at Kuluwan.

His reign lasted for two hundred and fifty years, others say three hundred years.

7   Then came Sultan Ayuma, son of Katur, son of Arsu.

His mother was Tumayu,

Daughter of Makamsi of the tribe of (Banu Gh. l.gh), (the Habasha).

And he also lived.

He died at T.t.nuri B.rangerya.

His reign lasted for twenty years.

8   Then came Bulu, son of Ayuma.

His mother was Ghat.djaya, daughter of Zakna of the tribe of Kay, folk of D.rangeq.

And he also lived.

When his end arrived, he died at Magh.djabadmi.

His reign lasted for sixteen years.

9   Then came Sultan Arku, son of Ayuma.

His mother was Aranges.na, daughter of San'ana of the tribe of Tamaghar,

Folk of (Kawar).

And he also lived.

One day, considering his numerous slaves,

He settled three hundred of them at D.rangeka,

Three hundred at the mosque of S.k.d.m,

And three hundred at Zaylan.

He died at Zaylan.

His reign lasted for forty-four years.

10 Then came Sultan (Hawa), son of Arku.

He had been invested by the Khalife.

And he also lived.

His mother was T.f.su, daughter of Arangekay.wan.n of the tribe of Tamagharange

He was very handsome

At his time, no one was more handsome than him.

4

Once, his daughter,

The daughter of Sultan Hawa

Entered his home at daylight

Dressed with seven garments to highlight her beauty.

That is why he had forbidden to all sultans' daughters from entering his home at
daylight.

When his end arrived,

He died at Ghanatkamana.

His reign lasted for four years.

11 Then came Sultan Abd al-Djalil, son of Ladsu.

His mother was Ab.li (or Ay B.li), daughter of B.q.ru of the tribe of Gh.m.z.m.

He died at Ghamazurida.

His reign lasted for four years.

That is all we (have written) know about the story of the Banu Duku; after that we
proceed with (writing) the story of the Banu Hummay who practise Islam.

12 Then came Sultan Hummay, son of Abd al-Djalil.

His mother was T.k.rangem, daughter of Gh.m.z of the tribe of Kay.

And when his end arrived,

He died in Egypt.

His reign lasted for twelve years.

13 Then came Sultan Dunama, son of Hummay.

His mother was Kitna, daughter of B.rma of the tribe of Tubu.

His horses amounted to (one hundred thousand

And that of his soldiers on foot to one hundred and twenty thousand,without the asakir

Among the Banu Hummay, no other ruler has been as mighty as he was.

It is said about him - may God have mercy on him -

That he had accomplished the pilgrimage to the Holy House of God at Mekka twice.

During his first journey, he left three hundred slaves in Egypt,

And did the same during his second voyage.

5

But at his third journey, when he went on board the ship,

The Egyptians thought that on his way back,

This king would conquer their country and add it to his domains.

For this reason, they decided to get rid of him.

Then they removed (the helm) from the ship

And he was drowned in the sea with his white garments,

So that from afar, he disappeared from sight in the sea of Prophet Moses.

The Most High had so decided.

May God have mercy on him.

His reign lasted for fifty-five years.

14   Then came Sultan Bir, son of Dunama.

His mother was F.sama, daughter of S.karam, of the tribe of Kay.

During his reign, he slew a thief.

His mother heard about that murder and asked him 'how dared you slay him,

When God - may He be blessed and exalted - had said "cut the hand of the robber?"'

For this reason, his mother put him in jail,

And he endured this situation for a whole year

When he decided to attend the council of the princes sitting in the courtyard,

His men cleared the place.

When the y left, the Sultan arrived and sat on his chair

When he decided to stand up, all the assembly did the same.

For this reason,

There is the custom between the Sultan and the princes which persists to day.

He died at Ghamtilu B.li Gh.na.

His reign lasted for twenty seven years.

15   Then came Sultan Abd Allah Bakuru

His mother was Zaynab, daughter of F.d.l of the tribe of (Tubu).

He was called Bakuru for the following reason:

When he was young, with prince Batku,

They went to Khayr.k.r.s.mu with their father Sultan Bir

Ghumsa F.sama, daughter of S.karam had received them with two hundred camels.

She had welcomed Bakuru with one hundred camels of the breed Bakuru,

Then welcomed Batku with one hundred camels of the breed Batku,

That is why he was given that name.

When his end arrived,

He died at F.f.s. May God have mercy on him.

His reign lasted for seventeen years.

16 Then came Sultan Salmama.

His mother was Aisha, daughter of Abd er-Rahman, of the tribe of Dabir

He was so-called because he was very black.

From Sultan Sayf to him, no sultan was born black,

But they were red like Bedouin Arabs.

His birth-name was Abd al-Djalil but because of his black colour,

He was named Salmama.

He was like that all his life.

When his end arrived,

He died at Dj.dj.s.ka Gh.z.runa.

His reign lasted for twenty-eight years.

17 Then came Sultan Dunama, son of Salmama.

His mother was Dabali, daughter of Batku, of the tribe of M.gh.rma.

And he also lived.

He went through the world (having to fight dissension).

He was the first to cut something called muni.

This thing was only known by God the Most High.

At his time, war started against Ghayu, son of L.f.rd,

And at his time, the sons of the Sultan were dispersed on different sides.

In former times, there were no factions.

And when his end arrived,

He died at Zamtam.

He had forty-one thousand horses.

His reign lasted for forty years.

18 Then came Sultan Kaday, son of M.t.la.

His mother was M.t.la, daughter of Yun.s of the tribe of M.gh.rma.

7

And when his end arrived,

He died at D.rya Gh.y.mutu, slain by ^can.d.k.ma Dunama.

His reign lasted for twenty-nine years.

19   Then came Sultan Bir, son of Dunama.

His mother was Zaynab, daughter (?) of L.k.m.ma.

He was Master of the World.

At his time two Fellata cheiks came from their country called Malli

When his end arrived,

He died at Shima.

His reign lasted for twenty years.

20   Then came Sultan Ibrahim, son of Bir

His mother was Kakudi, daughter of Sa ^ciduma of the tribe of Kunkuna.

He was the first to slay his son.

And when his end arrived,

Yerima Muhammad, son of Ghadi, threw him in the river at Zuzu,

According to what is said,

He was retrieved at Diskama.

King Abd Allah, son of Kaday and Fatima,

Then said to the people of the locality who had taken him out of the river,

'Come to me to be honored'.

And when they came close to him,

They were slain because they have seen the Sultan nude.

His grave is at Diskama.

His reign lasted for twenty years.

21   Then came Sultan Abd Allah, son of Kaday.

His mother was Fatima.

He was devoted to justice.

At his time, there a war between him and the king of Baghirmi Ghayu, son of
     D.rgh.z.na.

And when his end arrived. . .

He was told about four robbers, all sons of the same mother

He asked to bring them and he gave to his men the order to cut their throat.

For this reason,

The mother of the robbers prayed God to annihilate the descendants of the Sultan,

And God fulfilled her prayers.

He died at Djimi

His reign lasted for twenty years.

22   Then came Sultan Salmama, son of Abd Allah.

His mother was K.ma.

And he also lived.

When his end arrived,

He died at Yus.b in warfare against the Saw.

His reign lasted for four years.

23   Then came Kuri the Younger, son of Abd Allah.

And he also lived.

When his end arrived,

He died at Ghaliwa in warfare against the Saw.

His reign lasted for only one year

24   Then came Sultan Kuri the Elder

And he also lived.

He died at Ghaliwa in warfare against the Saw.

His reign lasted for only one year

25   Then came Sultan Muhammad, son of Abd Ajjah.

His mother was K.gh.la, daughter of W.rma.

And he also lived.

When his end arrived,

He died at Nanigham T.k.rgh.n in warfare against the Saw.

His reign lasted for only one year

26   Then came Sultan Idris, son of Ibrahim

His mother was Hafsa, daughter of Nasi

And he also lived.
When his end arrived,
He died at Djimi, other say Dammasak,
But the first indication is more accurate.
His reign lasted for twenty-five years.

27 Then came Sultan Dawud, son of Ibrahim.
His mother was Fatima, daughter of Nasi.
At his time, war started between the Sultan and his son (or sons).
And he also lived.
And when his end arrived . . .
He was the first to fight against the Bulala
And when his end arrived,
He died at M.l.f.la, slain by King Abd al-Djalil, son of Amiya.
His reign lasted for ten years.

28 Then came Sultan Uthman, son of Dawud.
And he also lived.
When his end arrived,
He died at Djimi in warfare against the Bulala.
His reign lasted for four years.

29 Then came Sultan Uthmanb. Idris.
His mother was F.mafa.
And he also lived.
When his end arrived,
He died at Djimi in warfare against the Bulala.
His reign lasted for two years.

30 Then came Sultan Abu Bakr Liyatu, son of Dawud.
And he also lived.
When his end arrived,
He died at S.f.yari Gh.rrna in warfare against the Bulala.
His reign lasted for nine months.

31   Then came Sultan Umar, son of Idris.

And he also lived.

When his end arrived, the war against the Bulala was at its climax.

He called for the Ulema and ask them 'what to do ?'

The Ulema answered 'Leave this place, the auxiliaries have disappeared'.

Then Sultan Umar moved with his army

And all his goods

And all the people

And went to Kagha.

So, up to today, none of our Sultans have succeeded in establishing his residence in Kanem.

And when his end arrived,

He died at D.magh.ya.

His reign lasted for five years

32   Then came King Said.

And he also

When his end arrived,

He died at Dakakiya because of the Bulala.

His reign lasted for one year

33   Then came Sultan Kaday Afnu, son of Idris.

And he also lived.

When his end arrived,

He died because of the Bulala.

His reign lasted for only one year

34   Then came Sultan Bir, son of Idris.

And he also lived.

At his time, there was a war between him and the <u>Kayghama</u> Muhammad, son of D.l.t..

And when his end arrived,

He died at B.gh.rmi K.n.n.tu.

His reign lasted for thirty-three years.

35   Then came Sultan Uthman K.l.n.ma, son of Dawud.
     And he also lived.
     He was dismissed from power by the <u>Kayghama</u> Nikali, son of Ibrahim and the
        <u>Yerima</u> Kaday Ka ᶜaku.
     He died at Afnu Kunu.
     His reign lasted for nine months.

36   Then came Sultan Dunama, son of Umar
     He also lived.
     When his end arrived,
     He died at Nanigham, killed (by his horse).
     His reign lasted for two years.

37   Then came Sultan Abd Allahb. Umar
     And he also lived
     At his time, there the war with the <u>Kayghama</u> Abd Allah D.gh.l.ma.
     The <u>Kayghama</u> Abd Allah dismissed him
     And appointed Sultan Ibrahim, son of Uthman at his place.
     He appointed him anew after the death of Ibrahim, son of Uthman.
     And when his end arrived,
     He died at F.m.l.fa.
     His reign lasted for eight years.

38   Then came Sultan Ibrahim, son of Uthman.
     And he also lived.
     He had never held a council,
     And had never visited the country himself.
     That is what is said about him.
     And when his end arrived,
     He died at Zamtam, slain by Kaday
     A man with the same name as the son of his father
     His reign lasted for eight years.

39 Then came Sultan Kaday, son of Uthman.
And he also lived.
At his time there was the war against Sultan Dunama, son of Bir
And when his end arrived,
He died at Am.za.
His reign lasted for one year

40 Then came Sultan Dunama, son of Bir
And he also lived.
When his end arrived,
He died at Aghaquwa.
His reign lasted for four years.

41 Then came Sultan Muhammad, son of Matala.
And he also lived.
When his end arrived,
He died also at Maza.
His reign lasted for five months.

42 Then came Sultan Amr, son of Aisha, daughter of Uthman.
And he also lived.
When his end arrived,
He died at T.rm.ta.
His reign lasted for only one year

43 Then came Sultan Muhammad, son of Kaday.
And he also lived.
He was very strict and redressed abuses.
When his end arrived,
He died at Maghdjib.d. N.ri Karburi.

44 Then came Sultan Ghadji, son of Imata.
And he also lived.
When his end arrived,

He died at Matakla Gh.m.r

Injured by the sword of <u>Kanema</u> Muhammad, son of Abd Allah.

His reign lasted for five years.

45 Then came Sultan Uthman, son of Kaday.

And he also lived.

At his time, there was the war between him and Sultan Ali, son of Dunama.

He was extremely generous.

And when his end arrived,

He died at M.k.da.

His reign lasted for five years.

46 Then came Umar, son of Abd Allah.

And he also lived.

He was not enthroned by the princes

And has wasted the heritage of Sultan Muhammad, son of Muhammad.

For this reason,

They all followed Sultan Muhammad, son of Muhammad,

With none of them having disobeyed him.

When his end arrived,

He died at Gh.m.t.l.rka.

His reign lasted for only one year

47 Then came Sultan Muhammad b. Muhammad.

And he also lived.

He was a strong and courageous sultan.

When his end arrived,

He died at B.r.b.r.dj.

His reign lasted for five years.

48 Then came Sultan Ali, son of Dunama.

And he also lived

At his time,

There was the war between him and Sultan Uthman, son of Kaday, who was slain.

After that, the fate was in favour of the Sultan.

Then, the war among the Banu Sayf was cooled.

And when his end arrived,

He died at Ghasrakmu.

His reign lasted for thirty-three years.

49 Then came Sultan Idris, son of Aisha.

And he also lived.

At his time, the war against the Bulala took a good course,

He defeated them and seized our town of Djimi.

His reign lasted for twenty-three years.

50 Then came Sultan Muhammad, son of Idris.

And he also lived.

At his time,

There was the war against Kaday, son of L.fiya, and he captured him.

Sultan Muhammad, son of Zaynab, settled nineteen years at Lada.

He was courageous, and the fate was favourable.

Under his reign, the kingdom reached its maximum extent.

He died at Ghasrakmu

His reign lasted for nineteen years.

51 Then came Sultan Ali, son of Zaynab.

And he also lived.

He was equitable and had never abandoned his equity all his lifelong to his death.

He died at Zamtam.

His reign lasted for only one year

52 Then came Sultan Dunama, son of Muhammad.

And he also lived.

At his time there was the war against Sultan Abd al-Djalil, son of the Ghumsa

There was also the famine B.wah.f.n.

He died at Ghasrakmu.

His reign lasted for nineteen years.

15

53 Then came Sultan Abd Allah, son of Dunama.
And he also lived.
At his time,
There was the famine Sima Adhadhu which lasted for seven years.
He died at Kitali.
His reign lasted for seven years.

54 Then came Sultan Idris, son of Ali.
And he also lived.
At his time,
There was the war against Sultan Abd al-Djalil, whose mother was the daughter of
Ghargur.
He re-established order in the kingdom,
And the country was prosperous.
He died at Alaw.
His reign lasted for fifty-three years.

55 Then came Muhammad, son of Idris.
He was of excellent temper, endowed with patience and modesty.
He died at D.kana.
His reign lasted for sixteen years and seven months.
He was so patient that he did not take sides in any controversy,
And at his time,
No one dared make trouble.
May God reward him.

56 Then came Sultan Ibrahim,
His mother was the Ghumsa of the tribe of Maghrama.
He died at Ghasrakmu.
His reign lasted for seven years and seven months.

57 Then came Sultan Al-Hadj Umar, son of F.s.ham.
And he also lived.

His reign is not singled out by anything special.

He died at Ghasrakmu.

His reign lasted for nineteen years and nine months.

58 Then came Sultan Ali, son of Al-Hadj Umar.

And he also lived.

He was a courageous man and a great scholar

At his time,

There was the famine Dala Dama.

He died at Ghasrakmu.

His reign lasted for forty years.

59 Then came Sultan Dunama, son of Ali.

And he also lived.

At his time,

There was a great famine which lasted for seven years.

He died at Ghasrakmu.

His reign lasted for nineteen years.

60 Then came Sultan Al-Hadj Hamdun, son of Dunama.

And he also lived.

His reign is not singled out by anything special,

The quietness and the psalmody of the Koran excepted.

He died at Ghasrakmu.

His reign lasted for fourteen years.

61 Then came Sultan Muhammad, son of Al-Hadj...

He also lived.

At his time, there was the famine Ali Shawa which lasted for two years.

He died at Ghasrakmu.

His reign lasted for sixteen years.

62 Then came Sultan Dunama Junior.

And he also lived.

At his time,

There was a great famine.

He died at Ghasrakmu.

His reign lasted for two years and seven months.

63   Then came Sultan Ali, son of Al-Hadj Dunama.

He was a wonderful sultan, unique, without equal at his time.

He had revived religion.

He died at Ghasrakmu.

His reign lasted for forty years.

64   Then came Sultan Ahmad, son of Ali.

A scholar himself; he was of good counsel for his fellows

He was profuse in giving alms, liked scholars and religion.

At his time, there was a general wellfare.

He worried about the fate of the poor.

He died at Ghasrakmu.

His reign lasted for seventeen years.

65   Then came Sutan Dunama, son of Ahmad.

Unique at his time, he surpassed all his peers;

He was a courageous man, excellent and of good counsel.

He died at Ngala.

His reign lasted for eight years.

66   Then came Sultan Ibrahim and his son Ali.

Both are dead.

May God be merciful for them.

This is the end of the story.

Part Two

The Genealogy of the Documents

Kanuri Domination and Literacy

Chapter 1

Collecting Historical Documents in Nineteenth Century Bornu

In order to grasp the importance of a historical document, it may seem useful to know more about its history: who was the author, what was his social position, who has been its guardian, how was it collected, what were the general socio-political circumstances at the time of the collecting, etc. This first part of our discussion will be devoted to a clarification of how H. Barth had succeeded in collecting important historical documents on Kanem and Bornu history in the 1850s. Incidentally, this clarification may be useful for assessing the importance of these documents for local people; and, more important, for the history of their society and the dominant paradigms of current historical scholarship.

Doctor Heinrich Barth was a trained German historian who has presented a doctoral thesis in history in 1844 on the Corinthian Trade (Lange 1977: 7, note 3). He was sent to North and Central Africa in 1849 under the auspices of the British government and his long expedition of exploration was certainly part of a programme of colonization of the African continent, which would take place few decades later. He arrived in Bornu twenty-five years after Major D. Denham, H. Clapperton and W. Oudney who had found the political situation of the kingdom a little confused with the weakening old Sayfawa dynasty residing at Ghazzargamo New Birni, and Mohammed el Amin el Kanemi, who had saved the kingdom from total collapse against the Fellata, residing at the new settlement of Kouka (Denham et al. 1826). Barth spent six years on this

21

expedition and Kukawa, the new capital of the kingdom of Bornu, was his main base camp. It was H. Barth who collected, directly or indirectly, two copies of the Diwan (Anonymous) and the Chronicle of the Bornu Expeditions of Idris Alauma (1564-75) written in 1576 by Imam Ahmad Furtu (Lange 1987: 13). These documents were given to H. Barth by some of his Bornu friends, but he had collected other historical information from other informants. It may be interesting to study the different aspects of this process of collecting historical data as detailed in the first chapter of the second volume of his monumental work (Barth 1965).

Barth (1965: 16) confesses that:

the whole business of collecting documents and information relative to the history of the old dynasty was most difficult and demanded much discretion, as the new dynasty of the Kanemiyin endeavors to obliterate as much as possible the memory of the old Kanuri dynasty, and has assiduously destroyed all its records wherever they could be laid hold of.

Obviously, giving historical information on the old dynasty to a foreigner was extremely risky for a subject of the nineteenth century Bornu kingdom. In order to strengthen its power and gain legitimacy, the new dynasty, fully aware of the importance of history, had implemented a policy of systematic destruction of the historical record. This socio-political context may partly explain why Barth had succeeded in having two copies of the Diwan from Shitima Makarémma, and two copies of the Chronicle from El Hadj Beshir ben Ahmed ben Tirab.

Barth had different informants among who some were singled out such as, Ahmed bel Mejud, an Arab from a division of the tribe of the Welad bu-Seb' a, living in the Wadi Sakiyet el Hamra in southern Morocco, who had travelled over almost the whole Western Africa, from Arguin on the ocean as far as Bagirmi, and has spent several years in Adamawa (Barth 1965: 35-6); A'msaka, a simple Kanemma chief who had formerly distinguished himself by his expeditions against the Budduma islanders of Lake Chad (Barth 1965: 39-40); Sherif Ahmed el Baghdadi, a native of Baghdad 'who had performed travels of an immense extent, from Khorasan in the East as far as Sansandi in the West, and from Tripoli and Morocco in the North as far as Asianti and Jena-Khéra and Fertit toward the south' (Barth 1965: 37); Bu-Bakr, a native from Hamdallahi, the capital of the Shaykh Ahmedu ben Ahmedu, who after the pilgrimage to the Mekka and a long sojourn in Yemen, was returning home (Barth 1965: 39), Agid

Burku, one of his pagan or non-Moslem instructors, and also hosts of the house of pilgrims, some of them native from Masena and Mali, belonging to Fulbe and Songhay ethnic groups.

The case of the Pullo (or Fellata) Ibrahim, the right-hand man of the Vizier El Hadj Beshir, holding the title of Digma, is very interesting. He claimed to be a 'son of the Sheikh el Mukhtar, in Kahaide on the Senegal, and cousin of the late Mohammed el Amin, the energetic prince of Futa-Toro' (Barth 1965: 35). A few years later, in 1870, Ibrahim was presented by Nachtigal (1980: 133) as a slave. 'From his long period of official power he had maintained a dignified bearing, which combined with his semitic appearance, would little match his slave status.' According to Brenner (1973: 76-80), after the execution of the vizier El Hadj Beshir ben Ahmed ben Tirab his former master, Ibrahim, as a royal slave, was transferred to the control of Abd er Rahman in 1853. But when Shaykh Umar was restored in power few months later in 1854, Ibrahim returned to his side as the most powerful of his palace slaves. Ibrahim has thus created an artificial 'pedigree' in order to be considered by the foreigner Abd el Kerim (H. Barth), as a full member of the Kukawa elite, an overt manipulation of his genealogy devised to fit into the local social system in the eyes of a foreigner. This episode is not to be considered as false history; on the contrary it is the 'real' history of individuals and people which shed some light on the contextual use of genealogies.

Two informants were considered the most important: the Vizier El Hadj Beshir ben Ahmed ben Tirab and Shitima Makarémma. The first, a Shuwa Arab, was the most important official of the kingdom after the king, appointed by Shaykh Umar in 1846 after the death of his father Mohammed Tirab at Kusseri on the shore of the Shari River, in a battle against Wadday troops called upon by partisans of the Sayfawa dynasty in their second attempt to take control of the kingdom. Shaykh Umar was much more interested in religion and learning (Brenner 1973), El Hadj Beshir was therefore the de facto ruler of the kingdom. In 1846, after the defeat of Wadday troops and the failure of the plot to otherthrow the Kanemiyin, a great slaughter of all the partisans of the old dynasty was launched, and the destruction of New Birni, the new city of the Sayfawa, was decided upon and carried out by El Hadj Beshir himself. 'From this time, people say, dated the great wealth of the vizier' (Barth 1965: 604). It is probably in these circumstances that the Chronicle was collected by the vizier as his part of the booty.

Mohammed el Beshir, being the son of the most influential man in Bornu after the Saykh, enjoyed all the advantages which such a position could offer for the cultivation of his mind, which was by nature of a superior cast. He had gone on a pilgrimage to Mekka in the year 1843, by way of Ben-Ghazi, when he had the opportunity both of showing the Arabs near the coast that the inhabitants of the interior of the continent are superior to the beasts, and of getting a glimpse of a higher state of civilization than he had been able to observe in his own country. (Barth 1965: 40)

In the atmosphere of intrigues in the high political sphere of the kingdom, El Hadj Beshir had to face the opposition of Abd er Rahman, the brother of the shaykh, backed by some members of the state council (Kokena). He also speculated on the rates of exchange of currency. His harem was a collection of 300 to 400 female slaves from different tribes and he was eager to add new 'specimens' at any time. He was also anxious to show how brilliant he was:

At such hours - late at night - I was sure to find the vizier or the shaykh alone; but sometimes they wished me also to visit and sit with them, when they were accessible to all the people; and on these occasions the vizier took pride and delight in conversing with me about matters of science, such as the motion of the earth, or the planetary system, or subjects of that kind. (Barth 1965: 60)

His major interest in reading the Chronicle of Imam Ahmed Furtu was to know if Djimi was really the former capital of the Ancient dynasty, to decide if it was worth launching a militatry expedition to conquer it. It is important to note that he did not allow his friend Abd el Kerim (H. Barth) to read the book even over his shoulder. El Hadj Beshir had many powerful ennemies among the officials of Kukawa - Abd er Rahman the brother of Shaykh Umar, many important members of the state council (Kokenawa) and numerous officials who were victims of his unlimited power - and was:

well aware of the danger threatening him, he was always on his guard, having sundry loaded pistols and carbines always around him, upon and under his carpet. Shortly before I arrived, an arrow had been shot at him in the evening while he was sitting in his courtyard. (Barth 1965: 43)

In 1853, Abd er Rahman succeeded for few months in seizing the throne. El Hadj Beshir fleeing to Wadday was captured by some Shuwa Arabs on the Shari River and delivered to Abd er Rahman at Kukawa after being promised that he would be granted a safe-conduct. He was, however, found guilty of treason, sentenced to death and strangled in December 1853.

Two copies of the Chronicle were made in April and June 1853 while Barth was on his way to Timbuktu (Lange 1987: 14). El Hadj Beshir himself sent one of the copies to the British Foreign Office during his last months in office and forwarded the other to be handed over to Barth on his return at Kukawa in December 1854, one year after his execution.

Shitima Makarémma had been a Kokenawa, a member of the state council under the old dynasty; 'he was the only man who was master of all the history of the old dynasty'. He provided H. Barth with two copies of the Diwan, which was according to him only a minor part of a more important book which was carefully concealed. He was a very intelligent old man but an 'acknowledged rascal', who had saved his life by his intrigues. For example, he had two daughters and succeeded in marrying one in each opposed faction, one to the Vizier and the other to Abd er Rahman (Barth 1965: 39). In December 1853, he too, but for different official reasons, was considered to have forfeited his life. He was arrested, tried, sentenced to death and executed with El Hadj Beshir the Vizier. It is not known wether Shitima Makarémma made both copies of the Diwan himself or had the work performed by one or two individuals; the differences between the copies, Memo H from Halle in Germany, translated, edited and published by O. Blau in 1852, and Memo L, today at London which belonged to H. Barth, lend some support to the hypothesis of two individuals.

For the Memo H to travel from Kukawa to Germany in the nineteenth century, to be translated and published in 1852, would have taken at least one and half to two years. This means that H. Barth had received the copies from Shitima Makarémma early in 1849 or 1850. If H. Barth had started to do some research on his own copy to check the historical accuracy of its content, it is possible that some members of the high political spheres of the kingdom may have been aware of the fact that he had received the information from the best historian of the old Kanuri dynasty, and that was certainly interpreted as an act of rebellion.

For different reasons, both men, El Hadj Beshir and Shitima Makarémma were executed at the same time by the same usurper, Abd er Rahman. This may have been a mere coincidence; obviously there were some sound political reasons for the death of El Hadj Beshir in such an unstable balance of power between fighting coalitions. His relationship by marriage to the usurper was not very helpful for <u>Shitima</u> Makarémma. It is difficult to escape the impression that it was the good relations of both men with H. Barth which were the link between these unconnected executions, and probably the fact that they gave important historical documents on the old dynasty which the Kanemiyin intended to destroy. This hypothesis is strengthened by the changing statuses of the Pullo Ibrahim. In this regard, it is worth noting the fact that the Kanemiyin not only initiated a programme of systematic destruction of the historical records related to the old Sayfawa dynasty, but also attempted to control the dissemination of historical information.

The way in which they began to communicate to me their information was in itself expressive of their respective characters, Ahmed (bel Mejub) protesting that, before he dared to communicate with me, he was compelled to ask the permission of the vizier, while Ibrahim laughed at him, declaring that he felt himself fully authorized to give me any information about Negroland. (Barth 1965: 36-7)

The kinds of historical information which may be given by a slave, albeit a royal slave, was certainly not really threatening for the ruling dynasty of the Kanemiyin; he was thus free to talk without constraints to the explorer. We may even dare say that, being the right-hand man of the Vizier, he gave frequent reports of his discussions to his master. The situation of Ahmed bel Mejub, an Arab traveller and learned man was totally different; genuine knowledge was a threat to the rulers of nineteenth century Bornu kingdom. <u>Shitima</u> Makarémma who had mastered the whole history of the old Kanuri dynastic was a major threat and that is probably why he was sentenced to death and executed by the usurper.

It is therefore suggested that there may have been different categories of historical documents: books such as the Chronicle of Imam Ahmed Furtu which were stored in the royal palace and which was taken by El Hadj Beshir as part of his share of the booty after the sack of New Birni, dynastic lists which were probably part of the libraries of courtiers and important officials and finally, the <u>mahram</u> which were royal letters granting privileges to state officials and courtiers (O'Fahey 1993). Collecting historical information and documents was probably a very risky task in the Bornu kingdom in the 1850s. For local people, it was not seen as a neutral quest for knowledge of the past, it was an integral part of the process of competition for ideological and effective control of power and political legitimacy.

Chapter 2

The Making of Rulers' Genealogies

Genealogies of kings or rulers are common features in the historical records in different kinds of societies (Freedman n.d., Henige 1971). In the southern part of the Central Sudan, dynastic lists and genealogies of rulers have been recorded among the Hawsa (Smith 1976), the Kanuri (Barth 1965, Landeroin 1911, Lange 1977, Nachtigal 1980, Palmer 1928, Zeltner 1980), the Kotoko (Lebeuf 1969) and the Shuwa Arabs (Zeltner 1977). When transformed through writing these genealogies lose an important aspect of what appears as their fundamental characteristic: rhythm. This characteristic became apparent to me during the 1991 archaeological field season when I was tape-recording the oral history of Houlouf, a Kotoko village settlement which was being excavated. Being unable to understand the local language, I was obliged to use an interpreter. However, I was struck by the rhythmic structure of the discourse and its musical poetry; it was something like a song known only by the oldest among the elders of the settlement. From this personal field experience, it appears that making genealogies was a kind of art, a specific kind of oral literature, or for short a genre littéraire. This kind of oral literature was used for different social purposes. It was one of the ways of linking the present to the past, transmitted from one generation to the next. Consequently, it was instrumental in the process of enculturation of the children but it was also functional in the sense that different claims could be supported by demonstrated and accepted genealogical connections with some prestigious ancestors. The contexts of use of genealogies were certainly very variable; families' genealogies may have been related at informal evening meetings in the courtyard and, depending on the social position of the families, some of the genealogies might be related at more formal and structured ceremonies such as rites of passage and ceremonies of enthronement of rulers and kings. In support of this proposal, it is clear from the data at hand that all the genealogies collected among the Shuwa Arabs by Zeltner (1977) are family genealogies, while those recorded among the Hawsa, the Kanuri and the Kotoko are dynastic lists of rulers. Data collected recently in different African contexts also supports the above hypothesis (Bonte and Conte 1991, Chrétien 1989, Njoya 1989, Okpewho 1979, Perrot et al. 1989, Schmidt 1978, 1983a, b, Zézé Béké 1989).

From the above discussion, it clearly appears that there were probably different kinds of genealogies; among the peoples without a centralized socio-political system, such as the Shuwa Arabs, the coexistence of both oral and written genealogies is attested; that was probably the case in all the societies of the southern part of the Central Sudan, but it is only written genealogies and almost exclusively dynastic lists which have been recorded by researchers. It seems almost axiomatic that with the formation of centralized socio-political systems, the making of lists of high officials, rulers and kings superseded all the others and became instrumental in the process of accession to offices, titles and kingship.

In African societies with centralized political regimes, the most important social position is that of the king or the ruler. In general, only members of one family have access to the throne. But in the majority of cases, whatever the kind of descent rules, matrilinear or patrilinear, it is the vote and not only the order of birth which decide for the successor. It is thus important for the candidate to the office to convince the voting members of the councils which make kings of their qualities as genuine heirs, the legitimation of his titles and claims can solely be based on historical arguments. (Boahen 1986: 256)

Considered from the above perspective, royal genealogies play a central role in the political structure of centralized social systems; they are a peculiar kind of constitution, subject to subtle alterations according to actual political and ideological circumstances. Kings and candidates for kingship were trained during their childhood to know their genealogies and did not really need them while they were ruling the kingdom. However, this 'constitution', the living memory of a centralized political system, may have been in the 'hands' of a learned man, acting as the curator of the regime and as teacher for the princes and future potential officials and rulers. It is in this context of teaching and popularizing the deeds of the ruling dynasty that the art of making genealogies was extremely important. A well-structured poem, a beautiful song, a rhythmic piece of literature was much easier to keep in mind. Such a piece of oral art is always in the making, it is never closed but always open to 'improvements'. This unstable nature of oral literature, which is congruent with changing social times, has not yet been fully acknowledged by students of the history of Kanem and Bornu.

Knowing the past to rule the present was the major purpose for making kings lists such as the Diwan; such lists played the role of political charts rather than that of archives, and this makes a tremendous difference. Ignoring this fundamental aspect of genealogies, be they oral accounts or written records, has caused serious difficulties and has hampered a deeper understanding of the multiple meanings of the Diwan of the Sayfawa dynasty, which have been reduced to the simple dimensions of chronicle of events (Lange 1977).

To the question 'why was the study of the past so esteemed and what sorts of value were ascribed to it?' A.F. Wright gave the following answers: 'one is that the successes and failures of the past provide sure guidance for one's own time. A second justification for history was . . . (that) to study history was to understand in clusters of concrete instances how men have fared when they lived in accord or defiance of the moral injunctions of the classics'. Ancient historiographers were thus invested with moral authority which no rulers dared ignore, precisely because this authority was based on knowledge of the past - namely, knowledge of the acting out and the consequences of these moral injunctions of the classics. (Chang 1983: 88-9).

The Diwan may thus be considered as one epic piece of oral literature among many others, reorganized and up-dated according to actual social, ideological and political circumstances and transmitted from one generation to the next. Thanks to the advent of writing and also to the efforts of many generations of researchers who have collected oral accounts, we have both written and oral genealogies of rulers which need to be studied as fluctuating and diversified historical point of views on the same topic: what is the best way to organize our society? The views according to which all the dynastic lists collected by different researchers are meaningless copies or series derived from an archetype, the 'original Diwan' which was lost forever (Lange 1977: 10) is misleading. This proposition is based on assumptions of homogeneous, harmonic society which are not supported by the historical evidence at hand; but, more important, it avoids asking the naive but fundamental question: Why make a dynastic list at all?

Concerning lists and geneaologies, it makes a difference to know who was attending the performance and the members of the audience. Were they recited during religious ceremonies, while giving offerings to the dead ancestors, following the requests of a colonial administrator representing a foreign power whose presence was used to lay claims for one's own lineage or territorial subdivision, with all possible means including the manipulation of genealogies, or were they performed after political independences for a researcher without any link with political powers - and in this case, was it preceeded by a libation to ask the forgiveness of the ancestors? These diverse circumstances are not without any effect on their reliability. (Perrot 1989: 14, my translation).

Chapter 3

The Advent of Writing

The earliest specimens of West African writing in Arabic have been found in Mali, at Essuk, Saney and Egef-n-Tawaqqast, in what appears to be the remains of the important market town of Tadmakkat and the ancient city of Kukiya, the first capital of the Songhay (de Morais Farias 1990), as epigraphs on tombstones. Some of the epigraphs gave the names of the individuals buried with their dates of death; these dates range from AD 1013-14 to 1182 or 1201. In Kanem and Bornu, there are no such records. The earliest written record is the book written by the learned jurist Masfarma Umar ben Uthman as a panygeric for his Sultan 'the just, godfearing, devout, brave, dauntless king, Idris ben Ali ben Ahmad ben Uthman ben Uthman ben Idris, the pilgrim to the sacred House of God' (Lange 1987: 34) mentioned by Imam Ahmed Furtu in his Chronicle written in 1571. Both sets of written records, the epitaphs from Mali and books from Bornu are directly linked to kings and rulers and religion. Writing and Islam had arrived in the <u>Bilad es Sudan</u> in the same package; the Moslem faith had therefore been instrumental in the dissemination of writing through what may be termed an education system (Barth 1965, Cuoq 1984, Fisher 1975, 1977, Lange 1985, Levtzion and Hopkins 1981, Lewis 1980, Nachtigal 1980, Smith 1976, Trimingham 1980). As religion, learning and literacy were strongly connected, it may be interesting to consider some aspects of these Islamic education systems which were and still are different from one area to the other.

In general, Islam had provided a strong cement crossing ethnic boundaries, backing and sometimes countering central monarchs. Throughout Africa, the elementary level of Moslem education was the Koranic school, with groups of pupils with their teacher sitting around a bonfire, under the shade of a tree or a shelter. 'The pupil's essential equipment was his writing board, on which were written portions of the Koran for him to memorize, or, as it might be in the case of longer passages, simply to learn to read fluently' (Fisher 1977: 322). In return, pupils often performed some work for their teacher and the Koranic schools were integrated into the framework of local communities, where they assumed the roles of initiation groups and/or age sets of traditional non-Moslem societies.

Beyond memorization of the Koran was the second main sphere of the traditional Islamic curriculum, in which the student learnt the Arabic language, and went on to work with subjects such as grammar, rhetoric, jurisprudence, logic, Koranic commentary, the traditions of the Prophet and the sources of the law. Such studies were usually centred on particular books. Each book would be read, sometimes even memorized; commentaries on the book would be examined; and the chain of authorities, from the original author or the first commentator down to the present teacher, would be learnt. After mastering each book, or subject, the student received from his teacher an ijàza, or license, indicating that the student himself was now competent to teach that subject to others. (Fisher 1977: 323).

The Moslem education system generated some specific patterns: the search for masters famous for their knowledge, movement of both pupils and learned men from place to place and the dissemination of Moslem scholars and their increasing influence in their respective communities. The system may be characterized as dissipative and wide-ranging as it often concerned teaching issues beyond the unique sphere of religious scholarship, as shown by the research of Kestelot on Epics of West Africa (cited in Okpewho 1979: 79).

The same apprentice will go in the morning to farm his master's land, and in the evening will be initiated into the secrets of a mystic tale or a *king-list* (emphasis mine). ... The education that the young African received in these workshops was thus a full and balanced education, aimed at a perfect integration of the individual into his group. . . a simple method of farming, or design in weaving, could give the master an opportunity to expound a myth of origin, similarly the epic of

Sunjata, for example, will be interrupted for a lesson in social psychology on the plight of a crippled man, or a lesson in botany on the use of baobab leaves; every subject of conversation or of observation is an opportunity for a digression, and every digression is an opportunity for an instruction'.

If we look at the Chronicle of Imam Ahmad Furtu from the perspective outlined above, the major purpose of writing it was certainly political and educational; its structure and syntax were devised to achieve the goal of educating the pupils attending the main Koranic school of Ghazzargamo, that of the Friday mosque. That school was probably in charge of the education of the children of the elite of the Kanuri capital. Bornu Koranic schools and scholars have been highly esteemed in the whole Central Sudan from the sixteenth to the end of the eighteenth centuries (Fisher 1975), and those from the capital city attracted pupils from the countryside. It is therefore possible to consider that the lessons learned and memorized at Ghazzargamo were disseminated all over the kingdom and in tributary states, and among these lessons there were probably the deeds and the genealogy of Sayfawa kings.

The Grand Imam Ahmad ben Furtu, of the tribe of Muhammad ben Mani, began the writing of this book on Sunday, when three days remained of God's month Radjab the Solitary in the city of Birni. We have not done this out of vainglory, false pretense, pride or the sake of fame, but in accordance with the obligation placed upon later generations to follow the example of their predecessors and to bear a likeness to the honorable - even though we ourselves are among the base. (Lange 1987: 34-5)

According to changing social and political circumstances, at the village, local and central levels of the kingdom, this knowledge was adapted to make sense of what actually happened. According to this point of view, it is the plurality of dynastic lists which is the normal state of affairs, and any single list is therefore meaningful and important because it may shed light on some unexpected aspect of a living and complex society of human beings, with their agreements, disagreements, disputes and peaceful relations.

Part Three

Contexts of Performance

Chapter 4

History versus Histories: Not One but Many Lists

There is not one but many dynastic lists: Memo H, sent by Barth to Germany in the early 1850s, was translated, annotated and published by O. Blau in 1852; Memo L, now in London, the personal copy of Barth, was selectively published with comments as Appendix L in the second volume of his journal (1965: 581-605), two royal lists also collected but not reported by Barth (Barth 1965: 15, 18) who specified that: 'I have not thought these two lists worthy of attention, except only with regard to the reign following that of the 58th king, if we count the reign of the usurper Said Ali, the son of Haj Omar. There are other lists published by Landeroin (1911: 346-51), Nachtigal (1980), that collected by P.A. Garcin at Bagara in 1971 in the Republic of Niger (in Lange 1977) and those published by Urvoy (1949), Palmer (1928), Cohen (1966) and Smith (1976) and finally the Diwan, a fusion of Memos H and L, translated and annotated by Lange (1977). All these documents deserve serious study but some of them, such as both royal lists collected by Barth, were lost (Lange 1977: 8, note 18), and the lists published by Urvoy and Palmer are considered as deriving from Barth's work (Lange 1977). However some interesting information pertaining to the art of making genealogies can be found. Barth (1965: 25) had observed that 'in one short list of Bornu kings which I posses, several princes are mentioned before Sef, whose names, such as Futirmi, Halar Sukayami, Halarmi, Bunumi, Rizalmi, Mairimi, have quite a Kanuri character.' The list which P.A. Garcin sent to Lange (1977: 9, note 22) was selectively reported and only names of kings congruent with the Diwan were published; this is unfortunate because that list seems to be very interesting. It was collected in 1971 in a former tributary zone of the Bornu kingdom; apparently people from that area did not seem to care that much about subtle differentiations between the ruling dynasties of Bornu, all the kings from the centre were considered en bloc from the beginning to the end of the sequence, a situation which is normal from the periphery. They had no particular interest, ideological, political or economic in having any kind of preference. Whoever was the king, they had to pay the tribute. It is therefore not surprising that it diverged from all the others collected within the geographic limits of Bornu, where political fractions and conflicting interest groups were in permanent competition. As observed by Lange (1977: 9, note 22), the list starts with twenty-four names of kings, both Kanuri and Arab, absent from the Diwan; followed by names of many kings (it is not specified how many) who have reigned between Hummay and Uthman ben Kaday. Three descendants of Kaday ben Uthman are then mentioned and the list ends with mentions of Shehu el Amin el Kanemi and five kings of his dynasty. The order of succession is similar to that of the Diwan and it presents features similar to one of the lost list of Barth, with Kanuri kings at the beginning of the sequence. The making of genealogies and especially kings lists is a highly political affair resulting from a complex pattern of social interaction (Chrétien 1989, Henige 1982, Njoya 1989, Southall 1970), as illustrated by the field experience of B.G. Blount among some groups of Luo speakers in East Africa. As an anthropologist, the above researcher wished to collect information about the genealogies of different lineages in his study area; some elders had more knowledge than others, but the most interesting aspect was that there were some missing links and major inconsistencies between different lists. Faced with this unexpected difficulty, the elders decided to organize a meeting to solve this vexing problem, and the researcher was fully confident expecting the problems to be solved easily. Contrary to his (and our) expectations, another and more interesting story has emerged:

The initiative and ability was based on speech prowess, knowledge of Luo history and folklore and social position among participants at the meeting and in the community at large. Combination of these factors yielded a genealogy that was a product of negotiation based on Luo history, but a history as a partially dictated and a partially arbitrated synthesis. In effect, the genealogies as history were created by the elders in competition, cooperation, and occasionally by fiat within a framework of Luo social interaction. (Blount 1975: 118)

It cannot seriously be believed that all these lists derived from one lost written archetype; if there was an archetype at all, it was probably contained within the canons of the art of making genealogies as part of a larger body of oral literature, which were transformed into written records in certain social, ideological and political circumstances. This study is based on the Diwan published by Lange (1977); theoretically, it may have been wiser to study both memos H and L separately, but they are not available as such. Both were given to Barth by Shitima Makarémma and their differences suggest that they did not result from copying the same original document. The copies were done by two individuals but it is not known whether Shitima Makarémma wrote one of them. There are many possible answers concerning the problem of the writing of these documents which need to be specified. Who did the work? When and where?

Barth (1965: 17) had answers to these questions. According to him, the various parts of the document were composed at different times, at the beginning of every new reign, with this official recording system starting under the reign of King Idris Katakarmabi, in the first half of the sixteenth century. According to this point of view, which is somewhat congruent with tightly organized bureaucratic regimes, from that time, a line or a paragraph was added to the record while the information pertaining to previous kings as derived from oral accounts. There are not only severe technical problems to overcome for this proposal to be considered relevant for the issue at hand - what was the medium, paper, leather, wood? - but also the plurality of lists is an argument against this proposal. For Lange (1977: 8) who agrees with the process of reporting dynastic information proposed by Barth, the writing of the Diwan had started much earlier, at the very beginning of the thirteenth century, but his arguments are weaker, as they are based on the so-called 'high precision' of information about the length of reigns, the patterns of kinship of kings, their burial places which, according to him, could not have been memorized for five centuries. As will be shown in this work, aspects of time, space, kinship, affinity, ethnonymy, etc. contained in the Diwan are much more complex and interesting than simple artifacts of limits of kingdoms, names of capitals and chronology of kings.

Paradoxically, the major obstacle in our attempt to know when the Diwan was written is Shitima Makarémma himself. We have to trust him when he said that the Diwan is simply a minor part of a more voluminous book, the 'Chronicle' which was carefully concealed (Barth 1965: 16). As he was the only man who was master of all the history of the old dynasty, his historical knowledge certainly covered the genealogy of Sayfawa kings and he was able to relate the whole story without difficulty. According to Barth, he was a very intelligent man, 'who had saved his life by his intrigues and at the same time an acknowledged rascal, to whom unnatural vices, which seem in general entirely unknown in these regions, were imputed' (Barth 1965: 39). Is such a character trustworthy? We are inclined to answer no, but that is not the most relevant problem. As sometimes happens in the field in the complex relationship between a researcher and his informants, it appears that Shitima Makarémma may have been disposed to say what was close to the expectations of Barth; for instance that there are very important historical documents but they cannot be seen because they are carefully concealed somewhere; pressed by Barth who was eager to satisfy his thirst for historical documents, he had decided to give few pieces allegedly coming from the invisible voluminous book. My proposals cannot be supported by positive evidence; but as far as the copies of the Diwan are concerned, it seems that the list of kings or at least fragments of genealogies were known by almost all educated members of the high political spheres of the kingdom. With his important knowledge of history, it was not very difficult for Shitima Makarémma to write a short document with five pages, and then use the service of a copyist to write the other one from dictation. Consequently, both copies of the Diwan were written in the 1850s, but the epic piece of oral literature upon which they were based was shaped long before, in the second half of the sixteenth century as will be shown later.

At this point of our discussion, a few examples will suffice to support the above hypothesis. According to the Diwan, the tenth king of the list, Sultan Hawa, son of Arku, had been vested with authority by the Khalife. His reign lasted for four years and, according to the chronology devised by Lange (1977: 67-8), that was in the eleventh century, from 1067 to 1071. This information raises some difficult historical problems if the Diwan is considered as an official record written according to the system proposed by both Barth and Lange. During the eleventh century, between 1060 and 1070, there were three Khalifes in the whole Dar al Islam. If those of Baghdad and Cordova are excluded from consideration as too peripheral relative to Kanem, it is only the Fatimid Khalife Al Mustancir from Cairo, who reigned from 1036 to 1094 (Cuoq 1984: 237), who could have invested Sultan Hawa. But according to Cuoq (1984: 238, note 664), no investiture by the Sultan of Cairo or even the Sharif of Mekka is known before the end of the fifteenth century. Instead of considering this information as a distortion of a genuine historical document, it suggests on the contrary that an ideological and political aggiornamento was under way in sixteenth century Bornu, and the past was reinterpreted accordingly.

The twenty-sixth king of the Diwan, Sultan Idris, son of Ibrahim and Hafsa, daughter of Nasi, who reigned for twenty-five years, from 1342 to 1366 (Lange 1977: 75), 'died at Djimi, some say at Dammasak, but the first indication is surer'. This passage shows clearly that the Diwan had been written from oral accounts but more important, the hesitation between Djimi and Dammasak has to be read within the context of competition between two competing factions of the ruling dynasty, the Idrissid and the Dawuddid, to state which of the factions deserves the credit or the blame for having started expansion in Bornu, or for having fled from Kanem. According to Imam Ahmed Furtu, it was the twenty-seventh king, Sultan Dawud, son of Ibrahim and brother of Idris, who moved with his people from Kanem to Bornu. For the Diwan, it is Sultan Umar, son of Idris who led the exodus, between 1382 and 1387, following Lange's chronology (1977: 76). It is worth noting that, according to the Chronicle of Imam Ahmed Furtu (Lange 1987: 43-57), Dammasak had been conquered during the first twelve years of the reign of Idris Alauma in the sixteenth century, approximately between 1564 and 1576, after a long and difficult military campaign. In the strictly historical, it may have been highly improbable for a Sayfawa king to be buried in an alien city, at Dammasak, about one hundred years before its conquest. The link between these series of events is clearly the name Idris and it is not surprising that the account of the military campaign against the Sau-Gafata and their settlement at Dammasak has been the first to be presented by Imam Ahmed Furtu in his Chronicle.

The third example concerns the nisba of the Sayfawa and more specifically the ethnic identity of Sayf ben Dhi Yazan, the founder of the dynasty. According to his pedigree, he belonged to the tribe of Banu Sakas or Banu Sakasak, his mother was from the Mekka and daughter of the king of Baghdad and had genealogical connections with the Quraysh. Al Qalqashandi later argued that this pedigree was in error because Sayf ben Dhi Yazan was in fact a Himyarit from Yemen.

There arrived a letter from the king of Barnu towards the end of al-Zahir Barquq reign in which the king mentioned that he was descended from Sayf ben Dhi Yazan. But he did not establish the genealogy, for he said also that he was of Quraysh, which is an error on their part, for Sayf ben Dhi Yazan descended from the tubba's of the Yemen, who were Himyarites.' (Levtzion and Hopkins 1981: 344-345).

This problem also poses serious historical difficulties. According to Lange (1990: 486-7), Sayf ben Dhi Yazan was a Yemenite hero who had expelled Christian Ethiopian invaders from Yemen during the second half of the sixth century (Rodinson 1961). He was also very popular among the Berbers of Northern Africa who claimed a Yemen origin. This popular hero had generated great devotion and esteem in Egypt on the theme of the fight of Arab Moslems against negro pagans. Popular stories were written on this hero in Egypt at the beginning of the fifteenth century and many earlier oral versions existed (Paret 1924 in Lange 1990: 487, note 87). Theoretically, it may be considered that the Sayfawa engaged in warfare against the pagan tribes during the formative period of the Kanuri kingdom in the sixteenth century, may have considered themselves as genuine heirs of the Yemenite Himyarite hero. It is therefore the ideological aspects of this amazing connection which is relevant in this context and not narrow historical accuracy in the academic sense of the word.

These three different examples support the hypothesis of ideological and political readjustment which took place at Ghazzargamo, the capital of Bornu kingdom during the sixteenth century. This aggiornamento was shaped in the form of epic oral literature which was, according to social circumstances, transformed into written record such as the lost Chronicle of the reign of Sultan Idris Katakarmabi written by Masfarma Umar ben Uthman, that of Ahmed Furtu on Idris Alauma, and the numerous kings lists among which are two copies of the Diwan.

Both examples discussed above lend some partial support to Barth's ideas concerning the period of maturation of the Diwan but his views were constrained by the historical research tradition in which he was trained and his assumptions about the organization of a state socio-political system. The presence of written records has been considered as the condition sine qua non for the making of history. It is therefore easier to understand why historical philology combined with Orientalism and Islamology have been so dominant in the historiography of the Bilad es Sudan, resisting the input of additional kinds of data from from other disciplines. Good ethnography, conducted in particular societies (Baroin 1985, Chapelle 1982, Conte 1979, d'Arbaumont 1989a & b, Lebeuf 1969, Reyna 1990) or in a wider cross-cultural perspective (Barth 1973, Bonte et al. 1991, Etienne 1987, Fortes 1969, Fortes and Evans-Pritchard 1967, Goody 1973, Leach 1973, Radcliffe-Brown 1950, Sahlins 1985, Southall 1970), is an important source of ideas which have generated genuine insights into the dynamics of societies of the recent past. Research in economic anthropology (Cordell 1985, Lovejoy 1986, Mauss 1990) offers important imformation on social organisation of production, distribution, exchange, and consumption of goods. The important development of studies on oral tradition and history (Goody and Goody 1992, Henige 1971, 1982, Perrot *et al.* 1989, Tyler 1978, Vansina 1985) is helpful in providing an inside and complementary view of historical process. It is probably one of the most helpful research strategies for avoiding ethnocentrism. Other disciplines, such as comparative mythology (Vernant 1974, Le Coran 1970), archaeology (Connah 1969a, b, 1971, 1981, 1984, Coppens 1969, Holl 1987, 1988a,b, 1989, Lebeuf *et al.* 1980, Schmidt 1978, 1983a,b, Treinen-Claustre 1978, 1982), palaeoclimatology (Grove 1985, Lowe-McConnell 1985, Maley 1981, Maley and Seignobos 1989), etc., offer additional points of view which also have to be seriously taken into consideration if we wish to improve our knowledge of societies from the past.

All students of the history of Central Sudan will certainly agree with the above assertions; however, integrating data from a wide range of disciplines is not an easy task and there will always be some problems concerning the peculiarities of each reasearch field. With these problems in mind, we will try in this work to bridge disciplinary boundaries in an attempt to provide a larger picture of the dynamics of Central Sudan societies during the first half of the second millennium AD, beyond the unending exegesis and commentaries on the classic Arabic sources as suggested by the following quote:

Ibn Furtu's inconsistent usage of technical terms often makes it necessary to reject a literal translation in favour of a translation which reveals the intended meaning. But no translation can guarantee full access to the original text. Any detailed study of the military culture of sixteenth-century Borno will have to be based on a philological analysis of the technical vocabulary not only of the K. ghazawat Barnu but also of the K. ghazawat Kanim. The examples given here may suffice to show that the technical terms used by the Imam Ahmad leave more room for interpretation than is at first apparent from the limited corpus of his writings. (Lange 1987: 23)

In this quote it seems to be assumed that there are some universally valid semantic standards for words, a real meaning buried under inconsistencies which have to be identified and discarded through philological exegesis (see Bonte and Conte 1991: 53 for a critique of this approach widely practised among Orientalists), without due consideration of the cultural milieu which may be partly accessible through a larger contextual study of the document as a whole, structured along some intelligible lines of thought which are not immediately accessible. There is no need to 'throw the baby out with the bathwater'; a rigorous scientific analysis of any piece of evidence is necessary, but the broader the approach encompassing different categories of data, the deeper will be our understanding of the issues at hand.

Chapter 5

The Skeleton of the Epic

If, as suggested by the discussion conducted above, the Diwan is considered as a peculiar kind of socio-political chart which wasshaped within the wider context of the emergence of the Bornu state or kingdom, it is not yet clear how these documents were organized, how their information content has been structured and how they are linked to the processes of state formation. These issues will be addressed in this chapter within a contextual and critical analysis of the Diwan translated and annotated by Lange (1977), and which will be based exclusively on what is <u>effectively</u> written in the record at hand; none of the corrections and improvements introduced by the translator will be taken into consideration at this stage of our analysis. The discussion will focus on attempts to reveal the syntactical and epic structures of the Diwan. In part four we will move on to the assesment of time, place, kinship, affinity, attribution of names, crises, warfare, etiquette and palaeoclimatic aspects contained in the Diwan, which appear to have been conceived as a contrasting, repetitive, sequential and overlapping network of political messages.

The Diwan is divided into sections and each section contains information on one king. The study of the frequency distribution of words within the whole document is based on the simple hypothesis that in order to achieve a rhythmic structure in a piece of literature which is not a simple narrative of events, due attention to number of words per segment is required. Incidentally, it may also be used as a yardstick to measure the length of enunciation of each segment and how they are related to each other. As this study is based on the French translation of the Diwan (Lange 1977), we are not sure that the results presented here will be the same as for the Arabic original.

The Diwan has sixty-nine sections, sixty-seven for kings, the introduction with the pedigree of Sayf ben Dhi Yazan or the nisba of the Sayfawa, and a paragraph of transition between reigns 11 and 12. The whole document was written in 3,723 words; the number of words in each section varies from 19 for the shortest (reign 5) to 204 for the longest (reign 13) (see Table 1). In simple descriptive statistical terms, the range is 185, giving a mean of 54.74, a standard deviation of 34.86 and a coefficient of variation of 0.63 (Table 2). The frequency distribution of words is highly skewed as can be seen in Table 1, with the longest sections concentrated among the first twenty-one sections of the document. If we exclude the nisba, the longest sections are concentrated between reigns 10 and 21. If we now focus our attention on the range of variations of fluctuations in the number of words per section (Table 2, Figure 1), it appears that the document is structured into four main sequences, excluding the introduction. Sequence I with ten reigns has 428 words (min. 19, max. 101, range 82, mean 42.80, standard deviation 22.81 and coefficient of variation 0.53); sequence II with fifteen reigns has 1220 words (min. 34, max. 204, range 170, mean 81.33, standard deviation 49.73 and coefficient of variation 0.61); sequence III with twenty-two reigns has 1021 words (min. 31, max. 79, range 48, mean 46.40, standard deviation 15.68 and coefficient of variation 0.33); and finally sequence IV with nineteen reigns in eighteen sections, has 744 words (min. 23, max. 70, range 47, mean 44.42, standard deviation 12.18 and coefficient of variation 0.27). From the coefficient of variation it appears obvious that the number of words in sections is more heterogeneous in Sequences I and II and more homogeneous in Sequences III and IV, an organization which may be metaphorically termed, from Chaos to Order, or from Darkness to Light. If the number of words in each section is equated with segmentation of the discourse (Figure 1), we have a bi-modal distribution of rhetoric segments in Sequence I (1-10); then four rhetoric segments distributed into three modes of decreasing importance in Sequence II (11-25), and finally in Sequences III (26-47) and IV (48-66/7) multi-modal (6 modes) and rhythmic structuring of shorter rhetorical segments. In terms of patterns emerging from the general distribution of word frequencies per sequence, it appears that sequences start with sections with steadily increasing numbers of words: 34 for section 1 in the first, 37 for section 11 in the second, 47 for section 26 in the third, and finally 64 for

45

section 48 in the fourth. This pattern may be congruent with an increasingly drama/tragedy-charged account of the fate and deeds of Sayfawa kings. It is also worth noting that, if we exclude the first section on Sayf ben Dhi Yazan the first king, we have almost the same number of words in section 2 (reign 2) at the very beginning of the account, and 66/7 at its end, respectively 24 and 23. It cannot be claimed that this abrupt and 'unhappy end' was based on the chronicler's ignorance of the events which accelerated the collapse of the old Kanuri dynasty in the nineteenth century, which are relatively well-documented (Brenner 1973, Nachtigal 1980). It is, therefore, a purposeful literary construct to close the story, meaning for example: 'Then, the cycle is closed.'

Obviously, even if the study of the frequency distribution of words starts to make sense, the Diwan is more than a collection of words; sections are written according to some relatively strict canons which shape the epic (Table 3). There are some invariant formulas which structure the different sentences in each section. Lange (1977: 17) has outlined four of them: the first one (F1), always situated at the beginning of the section, introduces the name of the Sultan: 'Then came....'. The second one (F2) ends the details on his kinship: 'And he also lived...'. The third (F3) introduces the place of his death or burial: 'When his end arrived, he died at...'. The fourth (F4), which mostly occurs in the last two sequences of the Diwan, introduces some major events of the reign: 'At his time...'. And the fifth (F5) indicates the length of his reign: 'His reign lasted for...'. These formulas are invariant in the whole Diwan, but all of them are not equally distributed in all the sections. Even so, they constitute the basic information blocks differentially distributed between sections or reigns among the sequences recorded in the document. As can be seen in Table 3, all the sections, with the exceptions of the nisba and the Transition, are introduced by F1; F2 is present in 45 sections, F3 in 57, F4 in 17 and F5 in 62 (Tables 3 and 4). The frequency distribution of all these formulas among the four sequences of the document is much more interesting. It thus appears that in Sequence I, F1 and F5 have the same frequency, F4 is absent, while F2 and F3 occur 5 and 9 times respectively. The same overall pattern of frequencies occurs in Sequence II. Sequence III presents equal frequencies of F1, F2 and F3 which are present in all the sections, while F4 is present in section 39 and F5 occurs 21 times. Sequence IV presents another frequency distribution, with F1 occurring 17 times in all the sections, equal frequencies for F2 and F3, 11 times, 16 for F4 and 15 for F5.

If we consider that in the narrative process, the meaning and the global intelligibility of sections, and then the whole account, is based on the successive accumulation of details contained in each information block, the arrangement of sections relative to each other, and the frequency distribution of information blocks may provide additional insight on the art of bards/performers. They may have been used as a rhythmic device, lengthening, shortening, equalizing, slowing and accelerating the tempo (Figure 2), engaging the participation of the attending audience, and generating the poetic and more generally aesthetic effects of the oral account being performed. In this regard Njoya's (1989) study of the songs performed at the Bamum royal court in Western Cameroon is very instructive:

They are shaped like monologue or dialogue which results in a general song which is recapitulated in choir by the audience. ... Often, they are epic accounts dealing with past events: wars, political crises, migrations, legendary figures, etc. These texts are also chronicles of the royal lineage or of the lives of some famous personalities. Their authors are very often the recipients of Bamum traditions. The members of different orchestras are for the most part leaders of secret societies or members of political, judicial and administrative institutions of the kingdom' (Njoya 1989: 67; my translation)

Beautiful musical compositions are welcomed by the audience and are instrumental in perpetuating the song. Musical beauty is the necessary condition for the survival of a song. This musical part is often very stable; it evolves very slowly. (Njoya 1989: 66)

The frequency of information blocks varies from 36 in Sequence I to 91 in Sequence III, with 50 for Sequence II and 70 for Sequence IV (Table 4). The recorded information blocks are combined in patterned succession (Tables 5 and 6). First, in terms of frequency distribution, three situations have been recorded in Sequences I to III, and four in Sequence IV. In Sequences I and II there are respectively 2 and 1 sections with two blocks, 4 and 8 with 3 blocks, and 5 and 6 with 4 blocks. Sequence III has 2 sections with 3 blocks, 19 with 4 and 2 with 5; while Sequence IV has 1 section, the last one, with 1 block, 2 with 3, 6 with 4 and 8 with 5.

As shown by the patterns of succession of information blocks, Sequences I and II are similar. Sequence III has its own pattern of succession in its three-block sections and shares the patterning of four-block sections recorded in Sequences I and II, and five-block sections of Sequence IV. It thus appears to be a sequence of transition between

47

different phases of the epic. Sequence IV has the greatest amount of diversity; while sequences I to III have three patterns of succession recorded, six have been found in this last Sequence, ranging from a section with only one block to one with five, with the series of four-block sections distributed into three patterns (Table 6). It is worth highlighting the fact that the Diwan ends with a section with one block, the shortest of the whole document, in which the lives of two kings have been condensed; as suggested earlier, this is certainly an efficient construct of the art of the performer of the epic to communicate to his audience the brutal end of the Sayfawa dynasty; and the gap with the preceding section, which has five information blocks is instrumental in achieving this aim

In this perspective, if the order of succession of information blocks is considered as resulting from a nested hierarchy of levels of meanings actually relevant for the performer of the epic and his audience, variations recorded in the different parts of the document start to make sense and cannot be reduced to artefacts arising from successive corruption, interpolations, and/or copyists' mistakes (Cuoq 1984, Fisher 1977, Lange 1977, 1985, 1987, Trimingham 1980). The narrative structure of the Diwan which emerges probably resulted from the combination of both Moslem and Kanuri traditions. It is very close to the annalistic form of early Moslem historiography described by Rosenthal (1968 in Wilks et al..1986), which 'as its name says, is dominated by the succession of the individual years - reigns in this case - under a heading such as "in the year *n* " or "then, there came the year *n* ", the various events of this particular year (reign) are enumerated'.

Part Four

Internal Analysis of the Diwan

Chapter 6

Numbers and Time Dimensions in the Diwan

Numbers play a crucial but ambiguous role in the Diwan; they are used to provide information on the succession of rulers, the length of their reigns and their might, wealth and power. The dimension of time is one of the crucial aspects of studying and making history; it is therefore logical that, confronted with the peculiarities of history-making in Black Africa, generations of historians were frustrated with the lack of written historical records and adequate chronological frameworks in local and indigenous accounts of the past. In this general context, the discovery of any fragment of written records was and still is an unexpected and providential gift; and if the documents collected happen to contain some chronological information, the fortunate researcher will try to use the data available as much as possible to build a more general chronology to make sense of the history of the area under study. This is exactly what happened with the Diwan, an amazing document which contains information on the length of reigns of different kings of Kanem and Bornu. But, as discussed previously, there are many dynastic lists and there are some important differences in the lengths of reigns of the same king in different versions; also, some reigns are obviously beyond the life expectancy of human beings, a feature also present in the lists of Hawsa kings. All these problems have generated interesting debates among students of the history of the Central Sudan and one of the solutions adopted by Lange (1977, 1985, 1987, 1990) to achieve an acceptable chronological framework has been to ignore the lengths of reigns of the first eleven kings recorded in the Diwan, to consider them as belonging to an earlier Zaghawa dynasty which was superseded by Hummay, the twelfth king, claimed to have

51

been the real founder of the Sayfawa dynasty. Surprisingly enough, it is only the total length of the reigns of these first eleven kings which has been discarded as irrelevant and above all connected to legendary figures, but other kinds of information such as toponyms, ethnonyms, the arrival of Islam, etc. are use to support the idea of an earlier Zaghawa aristocracy with possible Berber connections. Such an approach seems inaccurate because it misses the point: the Diwan is not a file containing the royal archives of the Sayfawa; the time dimensions of the document are social and symbolic and are framed within a specific kind of literature which needs to be understood before any attempt to translate them into calendar years.

Are there any patterns in the time dimensions contained in the Diwan? If the answer is yes, we should like to know how these patterns are structured and how they are related to each other. In the Arabic version of the Diwan, the lengths of reigns are reported in letters and not in numbers as is found in the French version at hand; this feature suggests that sound or rhythmic aspects may have been important for the performers of the narrative. This point deserves serious investigation which can be carried out with the collaboration of experts. However, as suggested by Crump (1992: 34-5), in any language, the word class of numerals has a fixed number of items which is learnt during the period of primary language acquisition; this property is shared with other linguistic classes such as prepositions, conjunctions and pronouns.

Using the linguistic term 'morpheme' to mean any non-reducible element in a language with its own recognised meaning, then the numeral lexicon is built up out of both unbound morphemes, consisting of all non-reducible numerals capable of standing alone, and bound morphemes, consisting of those elements which can only be used in combination. (Crump 1992: 35)

The linguistic aspects of numerals thus seem to be an important aspect of the Diwan, even if it has been translated into and written down in Arabic. Having no information on that interesting point with our flagrant lack of training in Arabic, we will focus on other facets of the time dimensions more easily accessible.

Three major aspects of time can be singled out from the record at hand: the chain of succession of kings, the duration or the length of reigns, and finally the total duration of the Sayfawa dynasty which can be inferred from the combination of both. The total duration of the Sayfawa dynasty varies from 1,472 years and 3 months to 1,522 years and 3 months because the reign of Katur, the sixth king is claimed to have lasted 250 or 300 years. The different reigns' lengths range from unstated duration (3 occurrences) to 250-300 years, giving a mean of 21.16-23.06, a standard deviation of 39.02-47.28, and a coefficient of variation of 1.84-2.05 (Tables 7 and 8, Figure 3). There are however important variations in the lengths of reigns not only from one king to another, but also between the different sequences of the Diwan which suggest something like a subtler pattern.

In Sequence I with ten kings there are two situations depending on the figure of the length of the reign of Katur, the sixth ruler under consideration, 250 or 300 years. In the first situation (Table 8: Sequence I), the ten kings reigned for 730 years altogether; the shortest reign, 4 years, being that of Hawa, the tenth king and the longest that of Duku and Katur, respectively third and sixth kings who reigned for 250 years; giving a range of 246, a mean of 73, a standard deviation of 90.04 and a coefficient of variation of 1.23. In the second situation, kings from the sequence reigned for a total of 780 years, with a minimum of 4 years, a maximum of 300 years (Katur), a range of 296, a mean of 78, a standard deviation of 100.51 and a coefficient of variation of 1.28 (Tables 7, 8 and 9).

It appears that in Sequence I the kings all reigned for periods longer than 15 years, with the notable exception of Hawa, the last ruler, culminating with reigns as long as 44, 50, 60, 250 and 300 years; this feature is congruent with pictures of a Golden Age, a time during which everything was peaceful. But also important is the fact that the lengths of reigns seem to be structured into successive sets of triplets of relative durations: triplet 1, 2, 3 with 20, 16 and 250 years, followed by 4, 5, 6 with 60, 50 and 250/300 years, and then 7, 8, 9 with 20, 16 and 44 years, the sequence ending with Hawa, the tenth king who reigned for only 4 years (Figure 3).

In Sequence II, with fifteen kings, the total duration of reigns is 279 years, with a minimum of 1 year for the three last rulers of the sequence: Kuri the Younger, Kuri the Elder and Mohammed, son of Abd Allah and a maximum of 55 for Dunama, son of Hummay, the thirteenth king, giving a range of 54, a mean of 18.60, a standard deviation of 15.18 and a coefficient of variation of 0.81. Ten reigns out of a total of fifteen lasted for 12-55 years, while five lasted for 1-4 years. It is worth noting that the series of the ten longer reigns are bracketed by two reigns, 11 and 22, which lasted for only 4 years, and that like the previous sequence, this one too ends with the shortest reigns of the sequence (Tables 7, 8 and 9). From the frequency distribution of reigns' lengths only, it appears that a new period of growth had emerged from the 'collapse' of the Golden Age, bracketed by two reigns of the same duration and ending with a new phase of collapse. The repetition of three successive reigns which lasted for 20 years each, followed by a sudden fall to a shorter reign of 4 years, followed in its turn by another repetitive succession of three reigns which lasted for only one year each is better considered as a narrative process to emphasize the dramatic charge of the account, similar to the strange calm which precedes a thunderstorm Sequence II may therefore be considered as the presentation of the Classic Period during which important social and ideological features of the system were laid down, with conflicting systems of values resulting in a chain of unpredictable and chaotic consequences: the thunderstorm which will threaten the very existence of the Sayfawa dynasty.

Sequence III with twenty kings lasted for 123 years and 3 months. In terms of total duration, it is the shortest sequence with the greatest number of rulers. The lengths of reigns vary from 0 (unspecified reign length), for Mohammed, son of Kaday, the forty-third king, to 33 years for the reign of Bir, son of Idris, the thirty-fourth king, giving a range of 33, a mean of 5.60, a standard deviation of 7.97 and a coefficient of variation of 1.42. In this sequence, there are only three reigns which lasted ten years or more (reigns 26 and 27 of Idris and Dawud, both sons of Ibrahim, and reign 34 of Bir, son of Idris). Eight reigns lasted from four to eight years, and ten others from 0 to two years (Tables 7, 8 and 9). The impression which emerges from the figures on lengths of reigns in Sequence III is that of a weakened system subject to major threats. It is as if the system had gone through a chaotic period of severe collapse which may be termed First Intermediate Period for reasons which will be clarified later. For the Sayfawa dynasty what may be considered as the hardest times during this First Intermediate Period occurred in two phases: the first from reign 27 of Dawud, son of Idris, to reign 32 of Said, considered as an usurper, and the second from reign 33 of Bir, son of Idris to reign 47 of Muhammad ben Muhammad. The figures giving shorter reigns succeeding one another at a relatively rapid pace is also a narrative artefact designed to support and communicate the feelings of threat and uncertainty provided by other and additional kinds of information.

Sequence IV with twenty kings, the last two being presented within a single section, lasted for 340 years. The lengths of reigns vary from 0 for the two last kings to 53 for reign 54 of Idris Alauma, son of Ali, the famous hero of Bornu history, for a range of 53, a mean of 17.89, a standard deviation of 14.44 and a coefficient of variation of 0.80 (Tables 7 and 8). In general, thirteen reigns out of a total of nineteen lasted 14 years and more; five from 1 to 8 years, and two in the same section at the end of the Diwan, 0. As shown in Figure 3, if we start from the last reign of the previous sequence, that of

Muhammad ben Muhammad which lasted for 5 years, there are in terms of frequency distribution of the lengths of reigns a series of four relatively coherent blocks of four to six reigns, apparent as successive modes which may be considered as lengths of string: the first one is 47, 48, 49, 50, 51 characterized by a sharp increase followed by steadily decreasing lengths of reigns 5, 33, 23, 19 and 1 year(s). The second is composed of 52, 53, 54, 55, 56 shows a bi-modal distribution curve with 19, 7, 53, 16.7 and 7.7 years. The third fragment of string, 57, 58, 59, 60 with 19.9, 40, 19 and 14 years shares the same distribution curve as the first, and the fourth, 61, 62, 63, 64, 65, 66/67 with 16, 2.7, 46, 17 and 8 years has a bi-modal distribution curve similar to that of the second string fragment. The alternation of the blocks presented above suggests the dynamics of the system at equilibrium with the successive replication of similar structural components based on the study of religion, knowledge of the Koran and the development of a structured state, the kingdom of Bornu; this part of the Diwan may consequently be termed as referring to the New Kingdom which had emerged after the turmoil of the First Intermediate Period, to end after 340 years with the murders of the last Sayfawa kings, Ibrahim and Ali and the rise in power of a new dynasty, that of the Kanemiyin, setting, for the supporters of the Sayfawa, the beginning of the Second Intermediate Period in the middle of the nineteenth century.

In the whole document, the general frequency distribution of reigns' lengths appears to be patterned according to sequences (Tables 9 and 10). If these reigns' lengths are partitioned into mutually exclusive classes, six reigns appear to have lasted for less than one year, from 0 to 9 months; such short reigns, belonging to class 1 (0-0.9 years) are absent from Sequences I and II and attested in Sequences III (four occurrences: reigns 30, 35, 41 and 43) and IV (two occurrences: 66 and 67). Twenty-six reigns belong to class 2 (1-8 years) with fifteen from Sequence III, five each in Sequences II and IV, and one from Sequence I. There are thirteen reigns in class 3 (10-19.9 years), two each in Sequences I and II, one from Sequence III and eight from Sequence IV. In class 4 (20-29 years) there are two occurrences from Sequence I, six from Sequence II, and one each in Sequences III and IV. The next classes, 5 (30-39 years), 6 (40-49 years), 7 (50-60 years) and 8 (250-300 years) have a total of twelve occurrences, five from Sequence I, four from Sequence IV, two from Sequence II and one from Sequence III. But more interesting, there seem to be two grand categories of patterned distribution of reigns' lengths among classes; discontinuous in Sequences I and II and continuous in Sequences III and IV. The pattern from Sequence I is strictly symmetrical, an exact replication of the same succession, something like an <u>ideal image</u>. In Sequence II the distribution is skewed with most of the reigns belonging to classes 2 to 4. In Sequence III with a continuous distribution pattern, reigns' lengths range from classes 1-5, nineteen out of twenty-two belonging to classes 1 and 2. Sequence IV shows an almost normal Gaussian distribution, with eight reigns out of twenty belonging to class 3; a pattern which mimics natural probability distribution (Table 9, Figure 4). The patterns discovered in this part of our discussion lend some support to our previous analyses and suggest the existence of a subtle and sophisticated system of selection of relevant numbers congruent with the socio-political nature of the messages contained in the different parts of the Diwan as suggested by the anthropological research on the multiple meanings of numbers in human cultural systems (Crump 1992).

Now almost any effective application of numeracy is tied up with the grasp of deeper structures, and one finds that the ability to remember what are essentially numerical positions is characteristic of the best performers in any relevant area - simply because they understand what these structures are. It is largely an economy of effort: a coherent structure, once it is understood, contains its own mnemonic base. (Crump 1992: 30)

It appears from our discussion that the lengths of reigns contained in the Diwan are far from being simple and straightforward chronological markers for the history of past societies of Central Sudan. This may appear at first glance, completely depressing for students of the history of Kanem and Bornu; but such an understanding is misleading because the major challenge is the study of past societies and an acceptable chronological control of the evidence may be achieved using other and complementary categories of data. Concerning the figures of reigns' lengths from the Diwan, they seem to be much more connected with numerology, that is symbolic meaning attributed to numbers which are accordingly constituted as a coherent system, which has been in the past an important part of mathematical and esoteric scholarship. Numerology also concerns the classification of all the world of human experiences into nested taxonomies. As suggested by anthropological research carried out among the Kotoko (A.M.D. Lebeuf 1969, J.P. Lebeuf 1976), numbers, and consequently numerology, play important roles in almost all aspects of social life; numbers are used to devise taxonomies for animals, plants, human beings and landscape: for instance, 1 symbolizes the prince, the principle of the unity of the community; 1,000 is the largest number possible, it is the number of the prince. Thus there are 37 numbers presented by Lebeuf (1976: 62-79) and considered to be very important by his Kotoko informants.

Numbers, which are always present in their minds, are never neutral for the Kotoko. The symbolism of numbers constitutes a coherent, rigorous and complete system which plays a permanent role in everyday life, in religion, and socio-political institutions. Numbers are charged with potency and qualities, and some relations established between some of them result more from intellectual associations and mythical equivalences than from simple arithmetical calculus; the same number, depending on the perspective adopted may change its 'value'. For example, both halves (*zala*) of Kotoko land, Halaka and Alage, are counted as 2 while the borderland of these regions, which is termed saï (i.e. single), is also counted 2, but 'another 2', because here, the internal partition between masculinity and feminity intervenes. (Lebeuf 1976: 59; my translation)

In his study, Lebeuf (1976) has shown that numbers, their rhythms and associations, are signs and movements which symbolize related functions, systems and ideas. Among the Kotoko, numbers are mythically integrated within the world, of which they constitute the essence, capable of expressing everything; it has been observed that they are intimately connected to power, socio-political organizations and institutions, to the ruler and his genealogy, the landscape, the spatial layout of the city and surrounding lands, to time, to religious activities in their very foundations and rites, to fertility, to human life, men, women and domestic life, and to classificatory systems encompassing edible grains, fishes, birds, wild animals, plants, crafts, metals, games, body adornment, etc. Numbers are therefore basically polysemic, they have many overlapping meanings. In this regard, the long-lasting attempt to translate the lengths of reigns of the Diwan into an absolute chronology has reduced the diversity of meanings of numbers, and it is probable that it is the less meaningful aspect which has been selected. Following the hypothesis proposed with regard to the lengths of reign given in the Diwan which seem to result from a subtle numerological system hitherto unknown, an exploration of this category of information may be useful.

The sample of reigns' lengths recorded in the Diwan ranges from a minimum of 0 to a maximum of 300 years; within this range, some thirty-four numbers have been selected and consequently, 264 have been discarded. A closer look at the distribution of figures on reigns' lengths (Table 10) shows some surprising patterning of selected numbers, as in class 2 for example, with a discontinuous succession of series 1-2.7, 4-5 and 7-8, the absence of any figure between 60 and 250, etc. It thus appears that some numbers may have had some special meaning and importance in the Bornu numbers system, as suggested by the following statement of Imam Ahmad Ibn Furtu: 'The excellence of equity is well known, its practice by a king for <u>one</u> day is equal to <u>sixty years</u> of worship; its mentioners are many' (Lange 1987: 35). In Ibn Furtu's accounts of the military expeditions of Sultan Idris Alauma, one is always the number of Moslems killed in battles against the pagans. Those Moslems were <u>de facto</u> martyrs of Islam. Surprisingly enough, within Kotoko numerology (Lebeuf 1976: 62 and 73), one symbolizes the king and the unity of the world and everything; while 60 represents the ideal length of human life and is also the number of silver rods present on the rings worn by northern Kotoko princes who were, according to Ibn Furtu, allies of Bornu during their wars against the Sao-Tatala. I shall not attempt to assign specific meanings to the numbers collected from the Diwan; the examples presented above simply aim to suggest that some numbers may have had peculiar symbolic meanings.

If we now shift from figures of lengths of reigns to all the numbers presented in the Diwan (Table 11), it appears that the numbers selected belong to a wider system containing additional figures such as 100 (two occurrences in reign 15 of Abd Allah Bakuru), 200 (one occurrence in the same reign), 300 (four occurrences, three from reign 9 of Arku and one from reign 13 of Dunama), 41,000 (one occurrence in reign 17 of Dunama, son of Salmama), and finally 100,000 and 120,000 in reign 13 of Dunama, son of Hummay. The range of figures attested in the section 13 that is, 2, 55, 300, 100,000, 120,000 encompasses almost the whole spectrum of the number system retrievable from the Diwan. It may have been used as a narrative device to support the importance of that king in the emergence and the development of the Sayfawa dynasty. It is also worth noting that the duration of famines attested in reigns 53, 59 and 61, is expressed using numbers of years, 7 and 2, congruent with the system adopted for the lengths of reigns.

If we compare the system of numbers inferred from the Diwan to that of the Kotoko adapted from Lebeuf's work, the most striking and strange thing which emerges is that both systems have thirty-six numbers with approximately the same pattern of distribution (Table 12). Nine numbers are present in class 1 (1-9); while the Kotoko set is a regular sequence of natural entire numbers that from the Diwan, which is discontinuous, achieves the same pattern through the addition of two fractional numbers, 2.7 and 7.7 if the lengths of reigns are considered in toto as one number only. However, it can also be argued that as these figures refer to years and then months, they are better recorded as two natural numbers, 2 and 7, and 7 and 7. Class 2 has seven numbers for the Kotoko set and eight for the Diwan one. From class 3 to 8, selected numbers decrease in general with increasing discontinuity. Class 8 is simply presented for convenience and includes all the numbers starting from 100; and even in such a dubious class, there is almost an equivalence between both numbers systems, with eight numbers in the Kotoko set and seven in the Diwan one (Figure 5). It is difficult to give a satisfactory explanation for this surprising convergence; but Kanuri and Kotoko have been in long-term interaction for at least one millennium and transfer of information and peoples have always occurred between both series of social formations. For example, among the Kotoko, the number 12 plays an important role in associations of ideas about the organization of political institutions. It is the number of the members of the council of elders which assists the prince in the government of his state, both at Makari, a former dependent region of the Bornu kingdom, and at Logone Birni. In the later ancient kingdom, there were twelve chiefs, in charge of the administration in the name of the Miarre, the prince. The number 12 also represents the total amount of the tribute in slaves and craftworks in mats, formerly paid each year to the Shehu of Kukawa, king of Bornu (Lebeuf 1976: 69-70).

At this point of the discussion, the time dimensions contained in the Diwan seem to be more connected to a deeper symbolic system than to problems of chronology. It thus appears that what has been interpreted as corruption of an original version of the Diwan, regarding the lengths of reigns, and even the omission of some reigns which were restored by historians are erroneous conceptions of the purposes of this important document. Concerning the length of the reign of Sultan Idris, son of Ali, the fifty-fifth king, better known as Idris Alauma, it has been changed to 33 years, even if it is indicated that:

Both Memos indicate a duration of 53 years. However, one can consider that the length of the reign of Idris Ben Ali which has been deleted, was added to that of Idris Alauma; because both kings had the same name. (Lange 1977: 81, note 6)

In the strict sense of historical sequence of events, the 'improvement' is accurate and welcomed, but does not explain why this occurred in this version of the Diwan. The structural consistency of the document as presented in this work is not seriously taken into account. If we now consider the different sequences of the Diwan as pertaining to a symbolic and ideological view of the deeds of the Sayfawa dynasty, Sequence I as the Golden Age, Sequence II as the Classical Period, Sequence III as the First Intermediate and Sequence IV as the New Kingdom, it appears that one of the most important king of the Classical Period was Sultan Dunama, son of Salmama, the seventeenth king, who has reigned for 40 years and destroyed the Muni, thus initiating a spiral of internal dissension and warfare which culminated in the abandonment of Kanem, the loss of Djimi and the long-lasting Bulala wars. After him, no other king reigned for such a long period. If my understanding is good, the reign of Idris Alauma is considered in the Diwan as the opposite of that of Dunama, son of Salmama. He put an end to the Bulala wars, reconquered Djimi, defeated a coalition composed of the descendants of Dawud with 'people of the rocks of Zabadu and the people of the rocks of Garasa, who were named Ngamo' (Ahmad Ibn Furtu in Lange 1987: 38), restored peace, order and prosperity. His reign was therefore singled out by a duration close to the ideal standards.

Chapter 7

Patterns of Distribution of Toponyms

Toponyms or names of places, be they names of localities, cities, capitals of state as well as ethnonyms, patronyms and titles are not given once for all; they are not 'culture-free'; they are part of social processes pertaining to the build up of a social landscape. As can be observed in multi-ethnic regional contexts such as the Cameroonian part of the Chadian plain, while inhabited settlements have names often agreed upon by almost everybody, uninhabited sites, de facto archaeological sites, are given names which differ from one ethnic group to the other; in this regard, names given to places are far from neutral labels. On the contrary, toponymy is a strategy to define a culturally relevant landscape, a behavioural space (Holl 1993a, b).

If read from the perspective outlined above, toponyms contained in the Diwan start to make sense (Table 13). In general, the names of places recorded in the document can be divided into four categories: the first category refers to countries, Kanim, in reigns 4 of Funa and 31 of Umar, son of Idris, Egypt in reigns 12 of Hummay and 13 of Dunama, Malli in reign 19 of Bir, son of Dunama, Baghirmi in reigns 21 of Abd Allah, son of Kaday and 34 of Bir, son of Idris, and finally, Afnu (Kano) in reign 35 of Uthman K.l.n.ma, son of Dawud. The second category refers settlements and/or kings' residences such as D.r.q in reign 8 of Bulu; Kawar, D.r.ka, S.k.d.m and Zaylan in reign 9 of Arku; Khayr.k.r.s.mu in reign 15 of Abd Allah Bakuru, the residence of Sultan Bir, Kagha in reign 31 of Umar, son of Idris and Lada in reign 50 of Muhammad, son of

Idris, which is the only explicit mention of a long-term residence of a king which lasted for nineteen years (Lange 1977: 80). The third category with two cases refers to important religious and political places: the Mekka, mentioned twice in reign 13 of Dunama, son of Hummay, and Zuzu and Diskama in reign 20 of Ibrahim, son of Bir. After his death, the body of Sultan Ibrahim, who had committed the horrible crime of killing his own son, was thrown in the river by the Yerima Muhammad, son of Ghadi; the corpse was later found by people from Diskama, where he was finally buried; but those who fished out the Sultan's corpse were found guilty of outrage against kingship and sentenced to death. And the fouth category of toponyms refers to places of death or burial of the kings; they are recorded for almost all the kings with the exceptions of Ibrahim, in reign 2, Arsu, in reign 5, Ibrahim and Ali, in reigns 66 and 67.

In Sequence I, toponyms refer to country (Kanim), settlements (five occurrences) and places of death or burial (eight occurrences); there is no reiteration of the same toponym in different reigns (Table 13), thus suggesting a kind of peripatetic court, moving from one place to another, a moving capital; the capital being were the king is settled.

In Sequence II, there are four references to countries, two for Egypt in reigns 12 and 13, one for Malli in reign 19 and the last one for Baghirmi in reign 21; one mention of a visit and a probable residence of Sultan Bir at Khayr.k.r.s.mu in reign 15, three important localities already presented above, and fourteen burial places (Tables 13 and 14). It is worth noting that there are two cases of reiterated toponyms: Egypt complemented by a mention of two Fellata pilgrims from Malli, to emphasize the connections with the Moslem world and Ghaliwa, to emphasize the fact that in reigns 23 and 24, two brothers, sons of Abd Allah (reign 21) with the same patronym, Kuri (Junior and Senior), were killed at the same place, Ghaliwa, in warfare against the same people, the Saw, in accomplishment of the curse of a woman, a mother whose four sons, charged with robbery, were unduly sentenced to death by the Sultan, the twenty-first king Abd Allah, son of Kaday, instead of the strict implementation of the stipulations of the Sharya which says that thieves have to have their hands cut off. The repetition of Kuri-Ghaliwa-Saw in both successive reigns may therefore be considered as a powerful narrative device to suggest increasing tragedy.

In Sequence III there is one reference to the country of Kanim (reign 31) in connection with the exodus to Kagha as a new and safer residence for the tormented Sayfawa, which is accompanied by three mentions of Djimi, sounding like complaints about the loss of an important settlement, and initiating a new phase of peripatetic moves from one place to another, supported by the mention of twelve different burial places for the next kings (Tables 14 and 15).

In Sequence IV there is one reference to a royal residence at Lada (reign 50); twelve out of twenty kings of the sequence have been buried at Ghazzargamo, the capital city of the Sayfawa, thus achieving the standard required for a 'genuine' state with the emergence of the New Kingdom.

The general distribution of toponyms (Tables 15 and 16) shows that reigns without any mention of place name are to be found in Sequences I and IV; the group of sections where one toponym is dominant, and their proportion increases from one sequence to the next: 5/10 in Sequence I, 11/15 in Sequence II, 20/22 in Sequence III and 17/19 in Sequence IV. It is as if the structure of the narrative had been shaped toward the idea of one centre for the social formation, Ghazzargamo. Series of reiterated toponyms starting in Sequence II, Egypt - Egypt (reigns 12-13), Ghaliwa - Ghaliwa (reigns 23-24), Djimi - Djimi - Djimi (26, 28, 29) in Sequence II, and Gasrakmu (9 times from reign 56 to 64) in Sequence IV, which is preceded by an alternating pattern Ghasrakmu - Djimi - Ghasrakmu - Zamtam - Ghasrakmu from reign 48 to 52, is certainly a narrative device to suggest the gradual achievement of the Bornu Kingdom of the Sayfawa. The brutal end of the Sayfawa is suggested by the lack of references to the burial or places of death of the last kings, Ibrahim and Ali. It can not be seriously claimed that this is an omission resulting from copyist's mistakes or even later corruption of the documents. The only explanation is therefore that this pattern results from intentional composition from the performers of the narrative later written in the middle of the 19th century. In the same vein, pairs of toponyms such as Baghirmi - Djimi in reign 21 of the cursed King Abd Allah, son of Ibrahim in Sequence I, Djimi - Dammasak and Kagha - Kanem in Sequence III, respectively in reigns 26 of Idris, son of Ibrahim and 31 of Umar, son of Idris, may also be understood as pertaining to a spiral of misfortune which had fallen on the descendants of Ibrahim who had committed the awful crime of parricide. Another series of immediate consequences, apparent in the toponyms of B.gh.r.mi K.n.n.tu in reign 34 of Bir, son of Idris, and Afnu Kunu in reign 35 of Uthman, son of Dawud, and interpreted as Kano in the Hawsaland (Lange 1977: 77, note 35(3)), is that, due to serious intra-dynastic troubles and competition for power, one king from the collateral line of Idris fled to Baghirmi while the other from the line of Dawud sought refuge at Kano, in Hawsaland. The patterns discovered in the distribution of toponyms may partly explain some major pieces of written records in the Bornu history. The lost Chronicle of

Masfarma Umar ben Uthman (Ibn Furtu in Lange 1987: 35) dealt with the Bulala wars and the conquest of Djimi by King Idris ben Ali ben Ahmad ben Uthman ben Idris, the forty-ninth king of the Diwan. The <u>Kitab ghazawat Barnu</u> and the <u>Kitab ghazawat Kanim</u> written by Imam Ahmad ben Furtu, respectively in 1576 and 1578, deal with the Bulala wars for the second and the Saw wars for the first (two chapters). Another piece of written record which was lost, also connected to the Saw wars, is referred to by Ahmad Furtu:

So when they became exceedingly hard pressed, they came in a great body to the sultan, acclaiming him, obedient and submissive, humbled and abased. They said: 'We are your captured slaves, the same as your slaves who are with you, who follow all your commands, in obedience; settle us wherever you like, in whatever place.' The Sultan that day stayed at the town of Damasak and said to the Grand Imam Ahmad, the author of this book: *'Write the names of all those people in a register.'* And they were brought to him and he wrote down the name of each one, singling them out one by one, and completed registering the names and counted themean. (Lange 1987: 49; emphasis mine)

The patterning of toponyms also lends some further support to the quadripartite structuring of the Diwan. One of the major problems which remains is that it is very difficult to assign all the places in which names are recorded to different known parts of the Central Sudan with some exceptions: Kawar, S.k.d.m interpreted as Segguedine in modern Niger, Afnu, Ghasrakmu, Alaw, Ghala, even Djimi is still controversial. For all the remaining places names, the attempt of Lange (1987:111-67) in his annotated gazetteer of identifiable toponyms is interesting but as yet inconclusive.

Chapter 8

Patterns of Distribution of Ethnonyms

Ethnonyms refers to name of groups of people. Anthropologists have offered different definitions of ethnicity emphasizing various kinds of characteristics (Barth 1969, Cohen 1969, 1974a, b, Dragadze 1980, Duncan 1981, Hjort 1981, Knutsson 1969). From these definitions, it appears that ethnic groups are characterized by shared world-views, language and a common territory. According to Dragadze (1980) for example:

Ethnos can be defined as a firm aggregate of people, historically established on a given territory, possessing in common relatively stable particularities of language and culture, and also recognizing their unity and difference from the other similar formations (self awareness) and expressing this in a self appointed name (ethnonym). (Dragadze 1980: 162)

As is often the case with definitions there are some difficulties with this one which does not consider some patterns of ethnonymity discovered in the field in Africa. Some groups have self-appointed ethnonyms, some others are called by names coined by their neighbours, others again have different names depending on the geographic areas and the differential distribution of ethnic groups, and more important, some groups may radically change their ethnic affiliation. In this perspective, ethnicity and its resulting ethnonymity are dynamic processes and instead of considering them only as sociological and anthropological categories, they are better conceptualized as social constructs. It is beyond question that ethnicity and ethnonymity are complex phenomena involving linguistic, territorial, historical, economic, political and psychological factors, but both are variables which in any socio-cultural milieu are interdependent with many others. Following Cohen (1974a: ix), an ethnic group can therefore be 'operationally defined as a collectivity of people who share some patterns of normative behaviour and form a part of a larger population interacting with people from other collectivities within the framework of a social system'. Any concept of ethnic group based on 'cultural content' alone is obviously not adequate as a research tool for the study of ethnicity in its various interactional contexts (Knutsson 1969: 99). It is only when ethnic distinction, stratification or differentiation are part of the individual's or group's strategies for preserving or increasing control of resources, social status or other values that a meaningful interpretation becomes possible. The relevant research perspective is then to concentrate on socio-economic and socio-political systems and treat ethnic ascription as one asset among several to have access to needed or attractive 'resources', be they subsistence niches, land rights, economic, political and symbolic power, etc. (Hjort 1981).

If considered from the research perspective outlined above, the series of ethnonyms recorded in the studied document which have to be understood in relation to the other aspects already discussed can be subdivided into three partly overlapping but distinct subsets contained within the socio-political domain (Table 17).

The first subset pertains to symbolic and ideological connections with the known Moslem world; it starts with the pedigree of Sayf ben Dhi Yazan, son of the daughter of the king of Baghdad and originating from the Mekka; he also belonged to the tribe of Banu Sakas or Sakasak and was connected to the Quraysh through one of his ancestors. The reference to the Habasha in reign 7 of Ayuma in Sequence I is meaningful in two contradictory senses with regard to the early history of Islam in the Arabian Peninsula. In the first, it can be considered to be linked with the episode of the first small group of the Prophet's followers from the Mekka, who being threatened by the Quraysh were advised to seek refuge in Ethiopia. In the second sense, it is linked to the fame of Sayf ben Dhi Yazan as Liberator of Yemen and victorious Arab over Christian Ethiopian and Black invaders in the first half of the sixth century AD (Rodinson 1961: 52-3). Then follows in Sequence II, references to the Egyptians in reign 13 of Dunama, son of Hummay, claimed to have been the first king converted to Islam and who died in Egypt, and the Bedouin Arabs, mentioned in reign 16 of Salmama, son of Bir, whose black colour of skin departed from the standard of the previous Sayfawa kings, presented as having been 'red'; and finally, the mention of two Fellata pilgrims from Malli, which may be interpreted as emphasizing the intermediate position of the land of the Sayfawa in the Muslim world (Table 17).

The second subset refers to the shifting and patterned strategies of alliance through marriages which started in Sequence I in reign 3 with the marriage of Duku, son of Ibrahim, to a woman from the Kay. Duku is later presented in the passage of transition between reigns 11 and 12 as the founder of the Banu Duku (Table 17). Obviously, the alliance between the first descendants of Sayf and the Kay which had started after two reigns (1 and 2), resulted in the emergence and the gradual formation of a new distinct social group which will later be labelled the Banu Duku. But before achieving this status and after three more reigns (4 to 6), the nascent social group had increased its alliance network by marrying a woman from the Banu Gh.l.gh in reign 7 of Ayuma, renewed its alliance with a new marriage with a lady from the Banu Kay in reign 8 of Bulu, and extended its network to include the Tamaghar in reigns 9 and 10, of Arku and Hawa respectively. In Sequence II, matrimonial alliance has been contracted with the Gh.meanz.m in reign 11 of Abd al Djalil, son of Ladsu. It is worth noting the fact that the father of this king is not recorded in the previous part of the Diwan, thus suggesting a shift which resulted in the emergence and the formation of a new and distinct social group labelled the Banu Hummay. This new nascent group had initiated a new process of alliances, with the Kay in reigns 12 and 14 of Hummay, son of Abd al Djalil and Bir, son of Dunama; complemented with the inclusion of the Tubu in reigns 13 and 15, respectively of Dunama, son of Hummay and Abd Allah Bakuru. In reign 16, with the 'unorthodox' black colour of the skin of the Sultan, his name was changed from Abd al Djalil (the same as the founder of the new social group) to Salmama; the name of his father is not recorded, thus suggesting a new shift in descent rules as will be discussed later. He had married a woman from the Dabir, followed in reign 17 by his son, king Dunama who had contracted marriage with a M.gh.r.ma lady, as did Kaday in reign 18. The ethnic ascription of Sultan Bir's wife, Zaynab, is unclear; there is a question mark after the mention - daughter (?) - followed by of L.k.m.ma which is interpreted by Barth to be the name of a tribe (in Lange 1977: 73, note 19(2)). In the Diwan references to ethnic groups are always preceded by 'of the tribe of '. L.k.m.ma is certainly the name of the father of the Sultan's wife and there is consequently no information on her ethnic ascription. Finally, in reign 20, Ibrahim, son of Bir had married a woman from the

Kunkuna. There is an interesting pattern which emerges from the network of alliance through marriages and the resulting distribution of ethnonyms: the Banu Duku (reigns 3 to 10) had resulted from alliances contracted with three ethnic groups, the Kay, the Banu Gh.l.gh and the Tamaghar, after a first delay of two reigns (1 and 2) followed by another of three reigns (4 to 6). A shift in the actual descent system occurred after reign 10, initiating the formation of a new group which may be termed a descent group, that of the Banu Hummay, which started with alliances contracted with another set of three ethnic groups - the Gh.m.z.m (reign 11), the Kay (reigns 12 and 14) and the Tubu (reigns 13 and 15) - in a continuous succession, a secular process in the socio-poltical system congruent with the normal social standards of the Classic Period during which the rise to kinship was based on alliances between four ethnic components. From reign 16 to 20 there are two shifts in the descent system with the references to mothers' names complemented by that of mothers' fathers and their ethnic ascription in reigns 16 and 18, respectively of Salmama and Kaday. This suggests the development of the matrilineal descent principle, probably backed by uxirilocal post-marital residence, as partly attested in reign 15 by the reception of Sultan Bir by his wife, the Ghumsa F.sama, daughter of S.karam of the tribe of the Kay, at Khayr.k.r.s.mu, and the present of 100 camels offered to each of the princes, Bakuru and Batku, who were named accordingly. For Salmama, this information is further complemented by the 'unorthodox' black colour of his skin, which set him a little apart among the descendants of Sayf ben Dhi Yazan. It can therefore be argued that the strategies of matrimonial alliances resulted in the development of factions which were highly instrumental in the development of the socio-political system at one period of its existence, but which, starting from reign 16 rapidly went out of control, becoming an increasing threat to the very existence of the Sayfawa dynasty.

The third subset refers to alien ethnic groups who had caused severe difficulties to the Sayfawa and killed many of their kings in warfare: the Saw, referred to four times, in a continuous succession at the end of Sequence II, from reign 22-25, followed by a break in reign 26 at the beginning of Sequence III, after which a new enemy appeared under the ethnic label of the Bulala. They are mentioned eight times in a continous succession from reign 27-33 (Table 17). The Bulala are further mentioned at the beginning of Sequence IV in reign 49 of Idris, son of Aisha, in a different context: 'At his time, the war against the Bulala took a more favourable course', emphasizing the fact that the New Kingdom will be that of peace, prosperity and learning. The Bulala wars did not cease, however, though the ethnonym was not mentioned again; instead, another narrative device was used to achieve the same aim in reigns 52 and 54; the narrator or the writer of the Diwan referred to 'Abd al Djalil, son of the <u>Ghumsa</u>' or 'Abd al Djalil, whose mother was the daughter of Ghargur'. This avoidance of the label Bulala lends further support to the notion of the Diwan as a genuine piece of oral and later written literature. The first and second subsets are overlapping while the third, which is relatively isolated and, starting from reign 21, characterized by the absence of any reference to ethnic ascription, is organized into two distinct and discrete series separated by reign 26.

Chapter 9

Patronyms, Gender, Kinship, Affinity and Rivalry

Names of persons recorded in the Diwan have played a crucial role in charting the genealogy of Sayfawa kings and their close network of kinship, affinity and rivalries. It has however been observed, almost from the beginning, that some persons, whether male or female, have Arabic names while others have local or Kanuri ones. It has also been noted that, according to different historical sources, each king has at least two patronyms, an Arabic and a local one. These interesting features, which have been explained in various ways, thus suggests that the performers and later the writers of the Diwan selected which of the attributed patronyms fitted the narrative of the Sayfawa chronicle. In this chapter, we shall attempt to present a model which makes sense of the different aspects of patronymy as recorded in the Diwan. In this regard, patronyms will be considered as 'social labels' geared to frame what are regarded as the major aspects of the identity of an individual as suggested by the passage on the reign of Sultan Salmama, the sixteenth king:

He was so-called because he was very black.
From Sultan Sayf to him, no sultan was born black,
But they were red like Bedouin Arabs.
His birth-name was Abd al Djalil but because of his black colour,
He was named Salmama... .(Lange 1977: 71)

Patterns of distribution of patronyms

The search for patterns in the distribution of patronyms can be implemented following two complementary lines of investigation: the first will consider the absolute frequency of names as they are iterated in each section or reign; the second will focus on the diversity of selected patronyms. Hypotheses concerning the possible 'meanings' of the patterns observed in terms of gender, kinship, affinity and rivalry will then be formulated and their accuracy evaluated. Patronyms also had thier own tonal qualities and, as word-units in the narrative with a particular phonemic structure, played a part in the general frame of the epic. This last aspect will be studied using only sultans' names.

Overall, there are 220 patronyms recorded in the Diwan as a whole (Tables 18 and 19). Their frequency distribution between sections varies from 1 (reigns 1, 24, 32, 56 and 62) to 10 (reign 15), for a range of 9, a mean of 3.38, a standard deviation of 1.87 and a coefficient of variation of 0.55. At first glance, variations in the frequency distribution between sequences are relatively moderate: ranging from 6-10 for the maximums, 5-9 for the ranges, 2.30-4.60 for the means, 1.05-2.30 for the standard deviations, and 0.40-0.50 for the coefficient of variations. Sequence II has the highest degree of variation, while Sequence IV has the lowest (Table 19). But on closer examination, the frequency distribution within each sequence shows some interesting patterns (Figure 6): in Sequence I there are two reigns' sets of equal frequency of four patronyms each; sets 2-3 at the very beginning and sets 8-9 at the end of the sequence. In Sequence II, there is one set of four reigns (11, 12, 13, 14) with four patronyms at the beginning, followed, after reign 15 which has the highest frequency of names, by two sets of two reigns, 16, 17 and 18, 19, the first with six and the second with four patronyms.

The distribution recorded in this sequence seems to refer to the implementation of some kind of 'normative behaviour' in the first part of this Classic Period which had later collapsed leading to the chaos of the First Intermediate Period. This is apparent in the frequency distribution of Sequence III, with, however, two sets of reigns at the end of the sequence, 40-41 and 44-45, with two and four patronyms respectively, which may be seen as unsuccessful attempts to implement new norms of behaviour. Chaos continued in the first half of Sequence IV up to reign 56, followed in the second half by the longest sets of equal frequency of patronyms, recorded in the whole document: sets 57, 58, 59, 60, 61 and 63, 64, 65, 66/7, with two names. This last pattern may be interpreted as referring to the successful implementation of new norms of behaviour.

Some patronyms are selected more often than others, the frequency of iteration varying from one (45 occurrences, Table 20) to seventeen (2 occurrences) for Dunama and Muhammad (Table 21). The different aspects of this process which may be inferred from the document under discussion present some interesting patterns which deserve a very close analysis.

There are 79 different patronyms and their distribution is overlapping among the four sequences of the document, some of them being subject to multiple iterations; 23 are recorded in Sequence I, 38 in Sequence II, 26 in Sequence III and 17 in Sequence IV. The sample of selected patronyms was widened from Sequence I to II/III and sharply narrowed in Sequence IV. There are some patronyms which are specific to some sequences while others are more widely distributed (Tables 20 and 21).

The recorded names can be divided into three categories: Arab, local or Kanuri and mixed names; and each category can be subdivided into female and male names (Table 22). The number of Arab names varies from 4 in Sequence I to 19 in Sequence III, with 11 in Sequence II and 12 in Sequence IV; while that of local names varies from 5 (Sequence IV) to 27 (Sequence II) with 19 and 6 respectively in Sequences I and III. In general, both categories show contrasting patterns of change (Table 23): the number of Arab names steadily increases while local ones decrease, a pattern congruent with the sustained expansion of Islam. The preferential selection of Arab names linked to the history of the expansion of the new faith may be expected as will be shown later. The frequency of females' names is almost the same from Sequence I to III, 8 to 10, followed by a sharp fall in Sequence IV, while that of males, which is always more important, varies from 15 (Sequences I and IV) to 18 (Sequence III) to 28 (Sequence II). In general, as far as gender is concerned, the ratio of female to male names, decreases from the beginning to the end of the document, this trend is neater and sharper for local patronyms (Table 23). It is worth highlighting the fact that among the 5 Arab female names, 4 are directly connected to the life of Muhammed the Prophet. Aisha was the name of the daughter of Abu Bakr and the second wife of the prophet; Hafsa was the name of the daughter of Omar ibn al Khattab, also a wife of the prophet, while both Fatima and Zaynab were names of daughters of Muhammed (Rodinson 1961: 356-72).

Among the forty-five single patronyms, 12 are recorded in Sequence I, 18 in Sequence II, 11 in Sequence III and 4 in Sequence IV. Most of them are local names, with the exception of eight (Abd al Rahman, Yun.s, Hafsa, Amiya, Abu Bakr Liyatu, Said, Matala, Amr and Imata) which are Arab. Excluding Said and Amr who were sultans, all the other patronyms refer to affines (mother, mother's father), allies, rivals and enemies. At the other end of the spectrum of the frequency of iteration of names, we have Dunama and Muhammad, both mentioned seventeen times each, starting from Sequence II, 5 versus 2 in Sequence II, 4 versus 10 in Sequence III and 8 versus 5 in Sequence IV (Table 21); the name Dunama, means 'Master of the World' in Kanuri (Smith 1976: 170, note 59), and thus appears to be the local and secular complement to that of Muhammad. To take another example, it may be very informative to track the trajectory of the name Abd al Djalil which is connected with the Bulala problem, a highly debated issue in the history of Central Sudan (Hagenbucher 1968, Lange 1977, 1982, 1987, Reyna 1990, Smith 1976, Zeltner 1980). The emergence of the Bulala had probably resulted from factional and conflicting processes within the Kanem socio-political system. In the Diwan, the Sultan of the Bulala is always named Abd al Djalil. This patronym first appear at the beginning of Sequence II, as the name of the eleventh king in the Diwan, son of Ladsu, who had initiated the development of a new descent group, the Banu Hummay. It is then mentioned in reign 16 of Salmama, as the birth name of this sultan which has been discarded because it did not fit to that person who departed from the actual normal standards. Abd al Djalil is again mentioned almost at the beginning of Sequence III in reign 27 of Dawud, son of Ibrahim, as king (Malik) within the context of warring Sayfawa factions and war against the Bulala. It is Abd al Djalil, son of Amiya who killed Sultan Dawud, the first Sayfawa ruler to be killed by the Bulala (Lange 1977: 75-6). In Sequence IV, the same name is mentioned twice: first in reign 52 of Dunama, son of Muhammad warring against 'Sultan Abd al Djalil, son of the Ghumsa', and second in reign 54 of Idris, son of Ali who had to fight against 'Sultan Abd al Djalil, whose mother was the daughter of Ghargur' (Lange 1977: 80). The patronym of Abd al Djalil thus shifted from the status of a Sayfawa sultan, to that of sultan's father, the founder of a new descent group, at the beginning of Sequence II, then as a birth name which has been discarded at the middle of Sequence II, thus transferring it to the rival factions where it was given to the Malik or king of the Bulala at the beginning of Sequence III and, finally as sultan of the Bulala in Sequence IV. The shifting aspects shown by the trajectory of this patronym is an abstract of the emergence of state formation, in competition with the emergent Kanuri state. The major difference between both emerging state formations lies in the processes involved in the development of each of them; it can be argued that after the beginning of factional wars between collaterals, each group was looking for new alliances. On the one hand, one of

73

the factions had succeeded in getting new alliance with speakers of Bongo-Baguirmi languages inhabiting the land situated along the Bahr el Ghazal and Lake Iro. They had adopted the idiom of their allies, had expelled the rival faction from Kanem, and had therefore been granted the new ethnonym of Bulala to emphasize the difference with the Sayfawa stricto sensu. On the other hand, the other faction had to seek refuge on the western shore of Lake Chad, and after a series of difficulties, succeeded in imposing its own idiom on the Chadic speakers of Bornu. The new society which emerged there was later granted the new ethnonym of Kanuri.

If we now narrow the focus and concentrate for a while on sultans' or rulers' names, it appears that all the ten patronyms of Sequence I are relatively short, with one monosyllabic Arab name (Sayf), seven bisyllabic: one Arab (Hawa) and six Kanuri (Duku, Funa, Arsu, Katur, Bulu and Arku), and two trisyllabic: one Arab (Ibrahim) and one local (Ayuma). The dominant voyels are A and U, a feature of the Kanuri language as attested in the whole document (Table 24).

In Sequence II, the phonemic structure of patronyms is relatively much more diversified with one monosyllabic Arab name (Bir) mentioned twice (14 and 19), two bisyllabic Local names (Hummay and Kaday); six trisyllabic names: three Arab (Ibrahim, Abd Allah and Muhammad) and three local (Dunama, Salmama and Kuri Junior and Senior), each of them being mentioned twice; one quadrisyllabic arab name (Abd al Djalil), and the longest patronym of the sequence of mixed Arab and Kanuri origin, with six syllabic units (Abd Allah Bakuru).

In Sequence III there are three monosyllabic Arab patronyms (Said, Bir and Amr), five bisyllabic names: four Arab (Idris, Dawud, Uthman and Umar, both later mentioned respectively three and two times) and one local (Ghadji), four trisyllabic names with three Arab (Abd Allah, Ibrahim and Muhammad (41, 43 and 47) and one local (Dunama - 36, 40), and three long patronyms, two of them of mixed origin (Abu Bakr Liyatu and Uthman K.l.n.ma) and the last a local one (Kaday Afnu).

In Sequence IV there are three bisyllabic Arab names (Ali - 48, 51, 58, 63 and 67; Idris - 49, 54; and Ahmad), four trisyllabic names: three Arab (Muhammad - 50, 55 and 61; Abd Allah and Ibrahim - 56 and 66; and one local (Dunama - 52, 59, 62 and 65) and the longest names are those of rulers who had been granted the prestigious title of 'El Hadjdj': El Hadj Umar and El Hadj Hamdun.

There appears to be an alternating distribution pattern of patronyms; Arab names are always mentioned at the beginning and the end of each sequence (Table 24). In

Sequence I, they are exclusively situated at both ends with Sayf and Hawa; in Sequence II names are distributed into sets: an Arab name, Abd al Djalil, followed by two local names, Hummay and Dunama, then another Arab name, Bir, followed by a mixed one, Abd Allah Bakuru, then a set of three local names, Salmama, Dunama and Kaday, followed by a set of three Arab names, Bir, Ibrahim and Abd Allah, then another set of three Local names, Salmama, Kuri the Younger and Kuri,the Elder followed by an Arab one, Muhammad. In Sequence III, local names are more and more dispersed, with only one set of two names, Kaday and Dunama, a trend which is amplified in Sequence IV with Dunama as the only genuinely local name. This pattern is congruent with the expansion and the development of a Moslem society in which the system of attribution of names to the descendants is progressively altered to include patronyms linked with the new faith, as shown by the ratios of Arab to local names through the four sequences of the Diwan which vary from 0.42 in Sequence I to 3.50 in Sequence IV, with 1.00 in Sequence II at equilibrium and 2.50 in Sequence III (Table 25).

In terms of frequency, Dunama and Muhammad are the more popular patronyms, recorded respectively eight and seven times (Table 26). Among the Arab names, those reminiscent of the early important figures of the initial development of Islam and its expansion into Syria and the Byzantine Empire such as the Prophet Muhammad, the four khalifes Rashidun: Umar, Abu Bakr, Uthman and Ali and the famous warrior Amr, have been preferentially selected. Among the Kanuri names, the patronym Dunama is used as the local complement to Muhammad, followed by Kaday which may be paralleled with turbulent Ali. The selection of patronyms recorded in the Diwan is therefore an important aspect of the kind of socio-political and ideological message delivered by the Diwan salatin al Barnu which is constructed and presented as the development of a genuine Moslem state in Bornu which is following the paths taken by earlier prestigious ancestors of the Dar al Islam

Patterns of kinship, affinity and rivalry

Kinship relationships are one of the most obvious aspects of the Diwan as they are the normal avenue to kingship. In Sequence I, the chain of descendants is unproblematic: all the fathers are recorded, eight mothers out of a total of ten are known as are seven out of ten mother's fathers ; the descent group of the Golden Age is thus clear with a system of patrilineal descent (Table 27). In Sequence II, a new descent group had emerged with Abd al Djalil, son of Ladsu, and lasted for five reigns (11 to 15). The fathers of sultans are known as well as the mothers and mothers' fathers within a system of patrilineal descent as noted for the previous sequence. With the sixteenth reign of Sultan Salmama, there is a shift which seems to suggest the development of a matrilineal system of descent and its coexistence with a patrilineal one resulting in the emergence of two overlapping descent groups. The first one with four sultans was initiated by Salmama (16) and included Dunama (17), Bir (19) and Ibrahim (20). The second had six sultans and was initiated by Kaday (18) with Abd Allah (21), Salmama (22), Kuri Junior (23), Kuri Senior (24) and Muhammad (25). With the sacrilegious act of Dunama (17) who had opened the <u>Muni</u>, problems started among the Sayfawa with the development of rival factions, a situation probably worsened by the fact that Dunama was the son of Salmama (reign 16) who achieved chiefship through his marriage with Dabali, the daughter of Batku, the brother of Sultan Abd Allah Bakuru (reign 15), contrary to the previous tight rule of succession from father to son.

In reign 21 and due to his misconduct towards four thieves who were sentenced to death instead of having their hand cut off as stipulated by the Sharya, an angry mother cursed the descendants of Sultan Abd Allah, and all four of them (22 to 25) were killed in warfare against the Saw; the descent group of Kaday was consequently totally annihilated. The system of alliance through marriages was also changed, as there are no further mention either of allied ethnic groups nor mothers' fathers, with the notable exceptions of Nasi in reigns 26 and 27, at the beginning of Sequence III.

In Sequence III, with the sets of relationships contained in both twenty-sixth and twenty-seventh reigns, the scene is set for the whole sequence. Idris and Dawud are brothers, both sons of Ibrahim (20); the mother of the first is Hafsa, a daughter of Nasi, and the mother of the second is Fatima, also a daughter of Nasi. The emphasis is explicitly on the strength of kinship relationships between both men on father's as well as mothers' side. Conflicts, murders and civil wars had however raged between both collateral lines which may here be considered as descent groups. The first descent group initiated by Idris (26) had ten sultans: Uthman (29), Umar (31and 46), Kaday Afnu (33), Bir (34), Dunama (36 and 40), Abd Allah (37) and Ali (48) at the very beginning of Sequence IV. The second, initiated by Dawud (27) had nine or ten sultans: Uthman (28 and 45), Abu Bakr Liyatu (30), Uthman K.l.n.ma (35), Ibrahim (38), Kaday (39) and Muhammad (43 and 47). Said (32) was an usurper; the situation of Muhammad (41), Amr (42) and Ghadji (44) are difficult to clarify in terms of belonging to one or the other descent group; but as suggested by the pedigree of Amr, 'son of Aisha, the daughter of Uthman', who may had have access to the throne through the marriage of his father with a princess, and the practice of an uxorilocal post-marital residence and matrilineal descent, these three sultans were probably members of one of the descent groups. Amr may have belonged to the Idris descent group as suggested by Lange (1977), but this connection is as yet unsubstantiated. More likely, he belonged to the Dawud descent group through his mother Aisha; if this was the case, both descent groups had the same number of sultans, ten each. Concerning the conflicts between both descent groups, the distribution of Arab and local patronyms can be read from another and complementary perspective; in this regard, in both descent groups, there are three sultans with local names: Kaday Afnu (33) and Dunama (36 and 40) in the line of Idris, Abu Bakr Liyatu (30), Uthman K.l.n.ma (35) and Kaday (39) in that of Dawud. They almost succeeded to each other in patterned sets: Abu Bakr Liyatu (30)-Kaday Afnu (33), Uthman K.l.n.ma (35)-Dunama (36) and Kaday (39)-Dunama (40). With the exception of Abd al

Djalil in reign 27 of Dawud, the outside rivals of the sultans of the line of Idris have Arab and mixed patronyms, Muhammad (34) and Abd Allah D.gh.l.ma (37), while those opposed to the sultans of the line of Dawud had local names: Nikali and Kaday Ka^{c}aku (35). These features seem to emphasize competition for legitimacy which may have been based, depending on actual circumstances, on local Kanuri or foreign Moslem systems of values.

The competition for power between the Idris and Dawud lines ended at the very beginning of Sequence IV with the death of Uthman, son of Kaday, killed by Sultan Ali, son of Dunama (48) and the descent pattern shifts once again to the matrilateral side with Aisha, mother of Idris (49), initiating the emergence of a new sub-line with the descent group of Idris. This new sub-line which may be considered as a descent group had seven sultans: Idris (49 and 54), Muhammad (50 and 55), Ali (51), Dunama (52) and Abd Allah (53); six out of seven sultans' fathers' names are recorded as well as two of mothers' names. The systematic absence of mothers' fathers' names as well as that of their ethnic ascriptions which started at the beginning of Sequence II, may suggest that these aspects of alliance were no longer important for the working of the socio-poltical system and the development of other kinds of lineage alliances based on preferential marriages which have been recently studied by some anthropologists and historians (Baroin 1985, Chapelle 1982, Conte 1979, Cordell 1985, d'Arbaumont 1989a, b). After the reign of Ibrahim (56) which is difficult to link to any one of the descent groups for lack of relevant information, another descent group composed of five rulers emerged with Sultan Al Hadj Umar (57), son of F.s.ham with Ali (58), Dunama (59), Al Hadj Hamdun (60) and Muhammad (61); all of the sultans' fathers' names are recorded. The last descent group which had been initiated by Sultan Dunama Junior (62), was tentatively composed of six rulers even if the fathers' names of the last two sultans have not been recorded: Ali (63), Ahmad (64), Dunama (65), Ibrahim and Ali (66/7). Patterns of descent are changing but they are preferentially patrilineal; but in general, the overall system seem to have been bilateral in nature. As suggested by Leach (1973: 56), in bilateral structures the practical economic - and we may add political - significance of descent through females is usually at least as significant as descent through males. He further specifies that the introduction into such a system of the kind of semi-patrilineal ideology which is associated with inherited patronyms generates an ideological differentiation, among the people concerned, between the value that is to be attached to patri-filiation and that attached to matri-filiation.

In his study on politics and marriage in south Kanem in modern Chad, Conte (1979) has shown the high incidence of lineage endogamy in the Kanembu social system; a feature which has also been noted among the Teda of the Tibesti mountain range in the 1950s (Chappelle 1982, d'Arbaumont 1989a, b) and among the Daza in modern Niger (Baroin 1985). According to Conte (1979: 277), the Kanembu view their society as cross-cut by three important cleavages (Kanembu / Haddad; freeborn / slave; master / dependant) which delimit partially overlapping, hierarchized social categories. These three important cleavages are further organized into vertical discrete lineages of a formally similar nature. He has further observed that the dominant ideology does not seem to explicitly recognize that the vertical fragmentation of kin-based political groups, based on the dual principle of the unilineal descent and the endogamic prescription, are essential mechanisms for the perpetuation of the stratification systemean A system which seems to prevent political alliance between subordinate sub-groups united by blood, marriage or clanship. '

Diachronically, a dual process characterizes the dominating/dominated relationship at all stages of the maximal lineage development cycle. On the one hand, forced endogamy and geographical dispersion maintain and accentuate vertical segregation between dominated groups as well as between dominated and dominant groups. On the other hand, nobles are free to reinforce horizontal segregation by manipulating tribute-exacting circuits, while being qualified to cross vertical barriers, especially through politically motivated interlineage marriages. (Conte 1979: 277)

The patterns of succession to sultanship which emerge from the genealogy of the Sayfawa rulers can be divided into four major kinds (Figure 7): the most frequent is that from father to sons which concerns twenty-seven sultans recorded in the Diwan, nine from Sequence I, eight from Sequence II, one from Sequence III (27 to 28) and nine from Sequence IV. The second kind is the succession of collaterals which is attested by the four sons of Sultan Abd Allah (22 to 25) at the end of sequence II. The third kind is the alternating succession in office of rulers from warring collaterals for at least three generations, as exemplified in Sequence III; if Said (32) the usurper is excluded, in the first generation four sons of Idris (29, 31, 33 and 34) had alternated with three sons of Dawud (28, 30, 35). In the next and second generation, three grandsons of Idris, Dunama (36) and Abd Allah (37), sons of Umar (31) and Bir (40), son of Bir (34) had alternated with two grandsons of Dawud, Ibrahim (38) and Kaday (39), sons of Uthman K.l.n.ma (35). In the third generation, three sons of Kaday, from the descent of Dawud, Muhammad (43), Uthman (45) and Muhammad (47) had alternated with Umar (46), son of Abd Allah and Ali (48), son of Dunama, from the descent of Idris. The same pattern of succession occurred at the beginning of Sequence IV for the sons of Muhammad (50) and Ali (51), both sons of Idris (49) who had reigned in successive pairs; with first, that of the sons of Muhammad, Dunama (52) and Abd Allah (53), followed by those of Ali, Idris (54) and Muhammad (55), thus initiating the transition to an ordered devolution of sultanship from father to son. The fourth kind is that of the rise in power of individuals of unknown pedigree, like Muhammad (41), Ghadji (44) and Ibrahim (56), through usurpation like Said (32) or through marriage like Amr (42).

Concerning the patterns of marriages, it is worth noting the fact that the female name of Aisha, that of the Prophet's second wife and Khalife Ali's mother's sister, is always associated with an important structural event. At its first occurrence, it is associated with the emergence of the Banu Duku, resulting from a system of matrimonial alliance with other ethnic groups listed in Sequence I. With its second occurence and as a princess, daughter of Uthman K.l.n.ma (35th ruler), her marriage had generated the rise to sultanship of her son Amr (42nd ruler) in Sequence III. And finally, in the third occurence, Aisha is the mother of Idris (49th ruler) who initiated the formation of a new descent group in Sequence IV.

The discussions presented above on the distribution of patronyms, gender, kinship, descent and rivalry show that a simple subdivision of the genealogy of Sayfawa rulers suggested by the Diwan between a so-called Zaghawa dynasty, the Banu Duku followed by the Banu Hummay is misleading if considered too literally. When the patterns of attribution of names, kinship, affinity and descent are considered, the system appears to be much more complex than suspected and shed some light on the dynamic process of formation of descent groups. Nine such descent groups can be inferred: one in Sequence I with ten sultans, three in Sequence II with six, four and six rulers, two in Sequence III with ten sultans each and three remaining rulers (Said (32) the usurper, Muhammad (41) and Ghadji (44), who cannot be assigned to any of the groups, and three in Sequence IV with seven, five and seven sultans, the corporate ascription of Ibrahim (56) being unknown. If seen from the perspective of the segmentation of the social system in the context of the expansion of Islam, the passage of transition situated between reigns 11 and 12: 'That is all we have written about the story of the Banu Duku; after that we proceed with writing of the story of the Banu Hummay who practise Islam', takes on a new meaning. It may be considered that the descendants of Sayf, the Banu Sayf or those of his tribe (qabilat), have been segmented into two branches (imarat or hayy); the hayy of Hummay was then segmented into three factions (Batn). The descendants of Ibrahim were at their turn divided into two warring factions and later those of Idris had formed three groups. If all these groups are termed Banu, we may have had at the highest level of inclusion, the Banu Sayf organized into the Banu Duku (1 to 10) in Sequence I, then the Banu Hummay stricto sensu (11 to 15), followed by the Banu Salmama (16-17, 19-20) who overlapped with the Banu Kaday (18, 21-5) in Sequence II. In Sequence III, derived from the Banu Salmama, there were the Banu Idris (26, 29, 31, 33-4, 36-7, 40 and 46) overlapping with the Banu Dawud (27-8, 30, 35, 38-9, 42(?), 43, 45 and 47), and finally in Sequence IV, deriving from the Banu Idris, and organized into three sub-factions, the 'Idrisawa' (49-55) followed by the 'Umarawa' (57-61) and, finally the 'Dunamawa' (62-67) (Table 28, Figure 8).

Chapter 10

System of Titles and Patterns of Events

The titles attributed to individuals, be they rulers, local and foreign rivals or even travellers resulted from a subtle combination of both Moslem and Kanuri cultural background. As will be shown in this part of our discussion, the titles system is intimately connected with the patterns of events as they are recorded in the different sections and sequences of the Diwan.

There are eleven different titles in the document, six are Moslem: Khalife, Sultan, Shaykh, Prince, King (Malik) and Ulema; while five are Kanuri: ꜥ.an.d.k.ma, Ghumsa, Kayghama, Kanema, and Yerima. With the notable exception of Ghumsa, all the titles are for males. In general, Moslem titles are iterated 95 times while local ones, most of them concerning rulers' rivals and enemies, are iterated only eleven times in Sequences II and III (Table 28). Khalife, the highest title after that of the Prophet in the Moslem world is mentioned only once in reign 10 from Sequence I, and pertains to the investiture to sultanship of Hawa. Even if in strict historical sense this event is highly doubtful as already discussed, it sheds some light on the local conception of a genuine Moslem political organization. Sultan is the commonest title used for almost all the rulers, with the exceptions of Arsu (5) and Bulu (8) in Sequence I, Said (32) in Sequence II and Ibrahim (56) in Sequence III. In Sequence IV all the rulers, whether they were actually in office, rivals (as Sultan Uthman, reign 48) or even foreigners (as Sultan Abd al Djalil, son of the Ghumsa, reign 52, and Sultan Abd al Djalil, whose mother was the daughter of Ghargur, reign 54), have been granted the title of Sultan. The title of Shaykh is used only once, in reign 19 of Bir, for two Fellata pilgrims from

Malli. The title Prince which is mentioned twice in Sequence II, has two overlapping meanings; in the reign of Bir (14) it is used as a generic term for all the courtiers, while in the reign of Abd Allah Bakuru (15), it is used in the narrower sense of sons of the sultan. The title of malik (king) which is mentioned seven times, two in both Sequences I and III and three in Sequence II, has two contrasting meanings. Used as 'king of the world in the four directions' as is the case for Sayf, the first sultan, or simply as 'king of the world' for Katur (6) and Bir (19), it has a positive meaning pertaining to the might and the power of the ruler. When used for foreign rulers, as attested in reigns of Abd Allah (21) and Dawud (27), respectively for the king of Baghirmi and King Abd al Djalil, and for the usurper Said (32), it has a negative tone (Lewis 1988: 84-8). The title of ulema, (Moslem scholar), is attested in Sequence III, in the reign of Umar (31); it is the ulema who advise the sultan to leave Kanem and start the exodus to Bornu; their contribution for the future peaceful and wealthy New Kingdom was therefore decisive. And finally, the prestigious title of Al Hadj, awarded to those who completed the pilgrimage to the Mekka, is mentioned six times: once in the nisba of Sayf ben Dhi Yazan, and five times in reign 57 (Umar), 58 (Ali), 60 (Hamdun), 61 (Muhammed) and finally 63 (Ali). The hierarchy of Moslem titles is relatively easy to grasp; the Khalife as the representative of the Prophet offered legitimacy to sultans. Sultanship is more related to mundane affairs and has both political and military connotations. The title of King has a dual meaning, but according to Lewis (1988) in early Moslem societies it has mostly a negative tone associated with tyranny.

There is in books on Moslem traditions, one hadith attributed to the Prophet Muhammad, in which we can find, in an ordered sequence of merit and preference, the list of some of the main titles of sovereignty currently in use by the Moslems. According to that tradition, the Prophet had said: 'after me, there will Khalifes, after Khalifes, Emirs, after Emirs, Kings, and after Kings, Tyrants. (Lewis 1988: 70)

In the Diwan, the intervention of sultans in matters of justice, in another sphere of competence, as attested by misplaced death sentences in reigns 14 and 21, is subtly condemned in the name of God: 'For that reason, the thieves' mother prayed God, asking for the annihilation of the descendants of the sultan and God fulfilled her prayers' (Lange 1977: 74). In this regard, the Diwan also contains some norms of behaviour which have to be fulfilled by the rulers.

Local male titles reported in the Diwan have been selected from a copious corpus of Kanuri titles and to quote only one example: 'the number of subordinate government officials is extraordinarily large, and in conversation with the inhabitants one is always running accross new titlles which owe their origin mostly to small districts or single villages.' (Nachtigal 1980: 256, note 1). The four titles selected are used for opponents to the Sayfawa rulers in Sequences II and III, Kayghama being the most important. According to Nachtigal (1980: 249), in nineteenth century Bornu the title of Kayghama was more and more forgotten. But in the old kingdom, it was the title of the most powerful official, the highest military commander of the country, who was always of slave origin. In time of war, he had supreme command of all the troops, but his role was insignificant during peaceful periods. The Yerima ranked next in power and was the title held by freeborn men and sons of princesses who exerted their authority on northwestern provinces of the kingdom. The precise meanings of all these local male titles in the Diwan is still unknown; if they were held by junior members of the ruling groups, they may shed some light on other aspects of the competition for power between factions with their shifting alliances.

In general, the diversity of titles increases sharply from 4 in Sequence I to 8 in Sequence II, and then decreases sharply again from 7 in Sequence III to 3 in Sequence IV, which, with the title of sultan for males and Ghumsa - the Queen Mother - for females, seem to pertain to the achievement of the ideal complementary pattern, a pattern supported by the sequences of reported events.

Numerous events are reported in the Diwan; they can be divided into three broad categories; peaceful and positive events, the harmful ones and those pertaining to conflicts and warfare.

Peaceful events are reported in Sequences I, II and IV (Table 29). They concern the colonization of new land and the maximum extent of the kingdom under Arku (9, Sequence I), Idris, son of Aisha and Idris, son of Ali (49 and 54, Sequence IV); norms of royal etiquette with the feature of avoidance between the sultan and his daughters in the reign of Sultan Hawa (10, Sequence I); the influence and power of the Queen Mother and the norms of behaviour of the courtiers in the presence of the ruler under the reign of Sultan Bir (14, Sequence II); the performance of the pilgrimage which is described in reign 13, indirectly indicated in reigns 12 (Sequence II) by the death of the sultan in Egypt and through the title of Al Hadj in reigns 58, 60 and 63 (Sequence IV); the reception of Sultan Bir and presents of camels offered to the princes Abd Allah

Bakuru and Batku by the Ghumsa F.sama in reign 15 (Sequence II); and finally the development of Islam, learning, peace and prosperity during seven reigns of Sequence IV (54, 55, 58, 60, 62, 63, 64). The majority of sultans of this sequence were trained in religion, some were scholars who gave wise counsel and were generous, giving alms to the poor as stipulated in the Koran in the famous Sura LXIV 'Mutual disappointment' given to Muhammed at the Mekka (in Le Coran 1970: 439)

15 Your wealth and your children are your temptation,
    whilst God holds in reserve a magnificent reward.
16 Fear God with all your might, listen and obey, give alms in your interest.
    He who is on his guard against his avarice will be happy.
17 If you make a generous loan to God, he will pay you back double;
    He will forgive you because he is grateful and longsuffering.
18. He knows things visible and invisible,
    He is the one powerful and wise.

Harmful events concern the exodus from Kanem to Kagha in reign 31 (Sequence III), famines reported in reigns 52, 53, 58, 59, 61 and 62 in Sequence IV and finally the sacrilege of Sultan Dunama in reign 17 in Sequence II who had opened the Muni. An event often overlooked in modern scholarship and which will be considered later.

Conflicts are reported in Sequences II and III; those from Sequence IV are mentioned at the very beginning in reigns 48, 49, 50, 52 and 54 were the final results of the events from the previous sequences. Of conflicts and disputes, four in Sequence II and nine in Sequence III, did not end in the death of one of the participants; five death sentences imposed by the sultan are reported in Sequence II, which resulted in the imprisonment of Sultan Bir (14) by his mother and the curse on the descendants of Sultan Abd Allah (21) by an angry mother; murders, parricide and regicide in intra-dynastic and civil wars and sultans slain in battles against foreigners, four in battles against the Saw (Sequence II) and eight in battles against the Bulala (Sequence III).

In general, the frequency distribution of events shows that Sequence I was basically peaceful. In Sequence II a dual pattern of peaceful versus conflictual events is attested (6 versus 23); in Sequence III, almost all the events reported pertain to conflicts and their consequences. Finally in Sequence IV, the pattern shifted to more peaceful events (12 versus 7) balanced by famines.

The fundamental event which initiated the reported cycles of difficulties for the Sayfawa rulers had been the opening of the Muni. This was probably an important symbol of the harmony of the society, and different and competing interpretations can be offered. If, as suggested by the hypothesis of the peripatetic capitals already presented and partially supported by the information from the Diwan, according to which the mother of Dunama (17) was the daughter of Batku, from the tribe of M.gh.r.ma, different tribes - or lineages - had different territories and alliances through marriage were instrumental in extending rulers' domains. Such ventures were probably sanctioned by exchange of presents and gifts, the performance of some rituals and ceremonies, and also by agreements or pacts setting out the rights and duties of the different partners. Such an agreement between different clans' heads may have been based on the mutual respect of actual social and religious practices of all the group members of the political alliance, and the Muni may have been the major symbol of peace and harmony between the partners.

If considered from a strictly political perspective, the opening of the Muni was a political upheaval of one of the allied clans. An example of such an agreement, a covenant between the Arna and the Tomagra, both Teda-speakers dating from 1889, was uncovered by Jean d'Arbaumont, a French officer, in 1950 and published in 1956 (new edition in 1989b). As this document shed some light on the dynamics of the Teda socio-political system at the end of the nineteenth century; it is worth considering it in some of its more relevant details for the issue at hand. The manuscript in Arabic has been given to d'Arbaumont by Sidi Allimi, the grandson of Sultan Ardea Bazeunmi, who was the successor of Derdey Kode, mentioned by Nachtigal as 'Kodda, headman of the Arna'. According to this short document: 'the Sultan, Amir of the Muslims, Ardea, son of Bazeun, was recognized as "paramount chief" during a meeting of eight elders and clans' heads, four Arna and four Tomagra' (d'Arbaumont 1989b: 13). Then follow the names of the delegates who had attended the meeting. The document defined the territorial extent of the authority of the new sultan, which comprised the land between Koufra to the surroundings of Abeche, and then stipulates regulations for the fines due in cases of abuses such as thieving, wounding, murders, etc. and the amounts due for payments of bride prices for daughters of the nobles - Maina - (Arna, Tomagra and Gounda) and those of free dependents - Meskin. The covenant also set the territorial boundaries for the different clans, distributing wells, wadis, dunes, hills and the highland of the Tibesti - Tarso - fields, palm-plantations, settlements, grazing lands, etc.

between both dominant clans: the land situated 'between the dunes - <u>Gueroud</u> - called Ourqua to the stony hills of Aremkar belong to the Arna for its right side, the left one belonging to the Tomagra' (d'Arbaumont 1989b: 15). Different clans' headmen of lower rank are also distributed between the Arna and the Tomagra command and are maintained in office:

the chief of the land of Kourou, Mohamed Arbeimi; the chief of the land of Kari, Agari Galmami; the chief of the land of Anni, Sokoi Kouni; the chief of the land of Koussi, Allei Ouarimi; the chief of the land of Miski, Dadi Mardaimi. (d'Arbaumont 1989b: 17)

The new sultan was vested with power to appoint new headmen and to remove the old ones from office if necessary. It is worth emphasizing the fact that the office of paramount chief alternated from one year to the next from one dominant clan to the other.

As suggested by our discussion of the above document, almost all the important and basic aspects of the socio-economic organization of these Teda clans are contained in this short manuscript; it is therefore highly probable that, before the advent of writing, such important pacts may have been symbolized by 'sanctified objetcs' included in the regalia of the actual ruling group. The <u>Muni</u>, 'that thing, only known by God, the all mighty' (Lange 1977: 72), was probably such a 'sacred regalia', symbolizing the political alliance between different ethnic groups and clans; an alliance which may have been renegotiated after each reign. The appointed paramount sultan may have been a <u>primus inter pares,</u> the first among equals, and his authority may have been based on a general consensus among the allied partners within a kind of loose confederation of tribes and clans. In this regard, the sacrilegious act of opening the <u>Muni</u>, which has to be considered in relation to the expansion of Islam, was a genuine socio-political disaster; it freed the partners of the confederation from their duties of obedience, prestations, mutual help, and probably also from the payment of tribute to the paramount sultan and, at the same time, it jeopardized the claims for access to paramountcy of the other allied groups. The opening of the <u>Muni</u> may therefore be interpreted as a '<u>coup d'état</u>' which unilaterally and radically changed the rules of the game; not surprisingly, it was immediately followed by the rise of rival factions, intra-dynastic and external warfare which threatened the very existence of the Sayfawa dynasty.

If now considered from the magico-religious perspective and in relation to the expansion of Islam, it can be argued that Sultan Dunama, the seventeenth ruler of the Sayfawa had initiated a policy of destruction of ancestral religions which contained diverse types of ancestors' shrines, secret places where important regalia were hidden, and a multiplicity of practices geared to ancestor worship and the manipulation of forces of the nature for the well-being of humans and societies. This attack on traditonal religions may have resulted in a general revolt of other partners and had initiated a series of internal wars.

Finally, the sacrilegious act of opening the <u>Muni</u> is better interpreted following a dual perspective combining political and magico-religious aspects; it was a violent attack on a key symbolic feature of the actual socio-political system and, as such, it initiated a long period of unrest for the members of the Sayfawa dynasty.

The period between the exodus from Kanem to Kagha, in what will be later called Bornu, up to the foundation of Ghasrakmu - Birni Ghazzargamo - the capital of the new kingdom, can be interpreted as that of the chaotic transition from one kind of socio-political organization, a loose confederation of dominant clans and ethnic groups, to another, a centralized state system, the kingdom of Bornu.

Part Five

The Early History of the Central Sudan in a wider Framework

Chapter 11

The Central Sudan: its Land and Peoples in Early Arabic Records

African historical scholarship based on the study and the exegesis of early Arabic records is a burgeoning field of research and we do not pretend, even for the less extensive records for Central Sudan, to consider all the kinds of information which constitute the usual parameters relevant for historians. This part of our study, which is based exclusively on the sample of Arab writers assembled, annotated and edited by Levtzion and Hopkins (1981), will focus on a narrow spectrum of issues relevant to contextualizing the propositions derived from the different interpretations of the Diwan; such issues concern the land, toponyms, peoples, ethnic groups, the rulers and the chronology of polities of the Central Sudan.

About Arab authors

Among the Arab or Moslem authors presented by Levtzion and Hopkins (1981), twenty-seven produced information on the Central Sudan; Sixteen were written in localities in the Middle East: Mesopotamia, Baghdad in Iraq, Ghazna in Iran, Damascus and Hamah in Syria, Merv in Turkmenistan and Cairo in Egypt; six worked in cities to the west: Marrakech in Morroco, Tunis in Ifriqiya, Cordova and Almeria in Spain; with three unknown cases (Table 30).

Most of the writers were scholars: geographers, historians or encyclopaedists; but a few were high officials, clerks from the administration, emirs, navigators and travellers. In terms of chronology, depending on the precision of the information, the sequence of authors ranges from 803-1490 AD. From c. 900-1000 all the written sources were produced from the east; a more balanced distribution for the provenance of the records came about in subsequent centuries. This pattern of distribution is interesting in that it shows how the geographic locations of the different authors, and their occupations influenced their writing and also their ability to have access to more reliable sources of information. For example the annual gathering of the pilgrims at the Mekka was a highly effective medium for disseminating all kinds of information about remote lands and peoples. The 'improvement' in the quality and the accuracy of information is not always correlated to time. None of the authors had visited Central Sudan; some of them named their informants: the traveller Ibn Fatima for Ibn Said (1214-69); a Kanembu poet Abu Ishaq Ibrahim b. Ya^cqub al Kanemi al aswad (the black) quoted in the biographical dictionary of Ibn Khallikan (1211-82); Uthman al Kanemi through Abd Allah al Saliliji for al Umari (1301-49); a letter from the king of Bornu from the sultans' archives in Cairo for Al Qalqashandi (1355-1418); some others have simply included extracts from previous works, etc.

Land Divisions and Toponyms in Central Sudan

Names referring to localities and land divisions have been used to support the idea of the prior existence of an earlier kingdom of the Zaghawa in the Central Sudan and to devise a chronology of the Kanem and Bornu states. The earliest reference to the term 'Zaghawa' is found in Al Khuwarizmi's (846-7) geographic description of the course of the Nile: 'It passes through the land of the Sudan and Alwa and Zaghawa and Fazzan and the Nuba and passes through Dunqula the city of the Nuba in long. 52° 20' and lat. 02° 00' beyond the first clime' (Levtzion and Hopkins 1981: 9). The Zaghawa are later mentioned in Ibn Qutayba's (889) account of the races of Sudan: 'The descendants of Kush and Kan'an are the races of the Sudan: the Nuba, the Zandj, the Qazan, the Zaghawa, the Habasha, the Qibt and the Barbar' (Levtzion and Hopkins 1981: 15). It is Al Yaqubi who first mentioned Zaghawa as a kingdom without cities, an idea quoted by Al Masudi (947); with Al Zuhri (1137), the picture is much more confused:

As for the Sudan who are beyond the Nile to the East, they are the Habasha; and those who are to the west of the Nile are the Nuba, the Zandj, the Janawa and beyond the Zandj are the tribe of the Sudan called Zaghawa. (Levtzion and Hopkins 1981: 97)

This confused description certainly attests to the author's poor knowledge of the area by the author (Table 31). The meaning of Zaghawa had thus shifted from being the name of a land, to a town, a people and then a kingdom (Table 32); but more often it has been used as an ethnonym. The same pattern occurred for the name Kanim, which is first mentioned in the work of Al Yaqubi dating from 889-90 (Tables 31 and 33). Bornu was mentioned later by Al Umari (1337-8) as land and subsequently as an independent kingdom (Table 34). Among the settlements, Kawar was mentioned as early as 871 by Ibn Abd al Hakam from Cairo, followed twenty years later by Al Yaqubi, from Khurasan; Djimi and Manan were mentioned by Al Idrissi (1154) and Kaka - or Jaja - by Ibn Said (1286-7) (Table 31). As far as the names of peoples are concerned it is the neighbouring peoples listed from one author to another which suggest some interesting observations: for all the authors writing from the Middle East, from c. 850-1000, the Habasha - Ethiopians - are given as the neighbours of the Zaghawa for the authors from Baghdad and Khurasan while for those writing from Cairo, it is the Kanim and the Nuba (Tables 32 and 33); later, from c. 1150-1450, for the authors writing from the Maghrib (Al Idrissi, Ibn Said, partly Ibn Khaldun who died at Cairo), the Kanim are reported as the neighbours of the Zaghawa, while for those from Baghdad, Hamah and Damascus (Yaqut, Abu l. Fida, Al Dimashqi), it is the Nuba or the Habasha. The effects of geographic location of the authors and the distance from the Central Sudan is patent in the above examples.

It is therefore suggested that the meaning of such terms as 'Zaghawa' in 850-1200 have to be considered as a generic term for all the black inhabitants of the Central Sudan beyond the Nuba, westwards, a loose grouping of all the speakers of Saharan languages. With the increase in trans-Saharan trade and movement of travellers and pilgrims there was an improvement in the quality and accuracy of information on Central Sudan.

As shown by a series of maps (Figures 9 and 10) there was successive change in the location of settlements and ethnic groups. In terms of location relative to each other, the distribution of settlements and ethnic groups presented in the map of Ibn Said and dating from the first half of the thirteenth century (in Lange 1985: 267) is congruent with that of the medieval Nubian kingdoms and the hypothesized sequence of Nubian migrations in the Nile valley (Adams 1982: 35, map 5 and 36, map 6). The land of the Nuba is situated on the east bank of the Nile, with Dunkula and Alwa on its shore; the land of the Zaghawa is situated on the west bank, with Tadjuwa, the city of the Tunjur, and Zaghawa as settlements in Section IV of the first Clime. The Tubu - Teda and Daza - are then located close to Kanem with settlements of Djimi and Manan in Clime I, Section III. Further ethnic groups and settlements such as the Kuri (from Lake Kuri), the Barabir (Berber), Djadja (Kagha or Jaja), Kawar, Tadmekka and Kawkaw (Gao) are also located on the map. The pattern of location of settlements and ethnic groups is clearly an East / West linear one. It shows that the Zaghawa were already located next to the Nuba, in the land that lies along the present-day Chad / Sudan boundary (Kropacek 1985). The idea of an early Zaghawa kingdom located in Kanem must discarded. However, this does not rule out the possible presence of few Zaghawa pastoral-nomadic tribes raoming between the Tibesti, Ennedi, Darfur and the Bourkou, in the Eastern part of the Chad basin.

Comparative Chronology

Dating the reigns listed in the Diwan is a difficult problem; the lengths of reigns, even if they are given in years, are not very helpful. Consequently, we will have to look for chronological information from external evidence (Lange 1989). The first relatively accurate chronological information can be found in the work of Ibn Battuta who had visited western Sudan in 1352 and 1353: he wrote that 'the people of Burnu are Muslims having a king named Idris who does not appear to the people and does not address them except from behind a curtain' (in Levtzion and Hopkins 1981: 302). The second is partly internal as it is a letter from the king of Bornu to Sultan Al Zahir Barquq of Egypt dating from 1391, in which the former was complaining about the exactions of the Judham Arabs:

As result of this dispute they have killed our king Amr the Martyr b. Idris, the son of our father Al-Hajj Idris son of Al-Hajj Ibrahim. We are the sons of Sayf b. Dhi Yazan, the father of our tribe, the Arab, the Qurayshite; thus we do register our pedigree as handed down by our Shaykhs..(Al Qalqashandi in Levtzion and Hopkins 1981: 347)

The third accurate chronological information can be found in the work of Al Maqrizi (1364-1442) who probably read the same document as Al Qalqashandi or used his work.

Their king in about 700 A.H/1300 AD was Al-Hajj Ibrahim of the posterity of Sayf b. Dhi Yazan. He held the throne of Kanimean Kanim is the throne of Barnu. There ruled after him his son Al-Hajj Idris, then his brother Da'ud b. Ibrahim, then 'Umar the son of his brother Al-Hajj Idris, then his brother 'Uthman b. Idris who ruled a little before 800 A.H/1397-8 AD. The people of Kanim then rose against them and apostatized and.... They are Muslims and wage Holy War on the people of Kanim They have twelve kingdoms. (Al Maqrizi in Levtzion and Hopkins 1981: 355).

Even if there are some disagreement between researchers (Barth 1965, Brenner 1973, Denham *et al.* 1826, Lange 1977, Nachtigal 1980, Smith 1976), the chronology of the last reigns of the Sayfawa dynasty recorded in the version of the Diwan under discussion here, those of Ahmad b. Ali (64), Dunama b. Ahmad (65), Ibrahim (66) and Ali b. Ibrahim (67) is relatively well established. Sultan Dunama b. Ahmad was slain in 1820 at Ngala fighting against Baghirmi troops; Sultan Ibrahim was executed in May 1846 by the Kanemiyin as was his son, Sultan Ali, few years later in the 1850s. From the three Arabic sources presented above, we have a relatively converging series of dates on the same chronological sequence; other chronological information is presented and discussed in Lange (1977: 113-54), especially those pertaining to the advent of Islam and the earliest rulers contained in works of Ibn Said and Al Maqrizi:

The first of their kings to adopt Islam was Muhammad b. Jabal b. ʾAbd Allah b. ʾUthman b. Muhammad b. They assert that he is descended from Sayf b. Dhi Yazan and that between the two there were about 40 kings' (in Hopkins and Levtzion 1981: 353).

Reconsidered by Lange (1977: 137, my translation), this set of information is presented as follows: 'The first of their kings to convert to Islam was Muhammad (= Dunama) b. Djabl (read: Djil = cAbd al Djalil = Salmama b. cAbd Allah b cUthman (= Bir) b. Muhammad (= Dunama) b. Umi (or Ami) (= Hummay) ...'. The blank left by Al Maqrizi is filled with the name of Hummay; the strict correspondence made between names is considered relevant for the issue of the advent of Islam. One can but wonder why such a correspondence is not true for all the later periods. It can simply be argued that this exercise is far from convincing, the research problem being solved before it is even framed in adequate terms. But more important, this information seems to have been transmitted to Al Maqrizi in Cairo by a Kanembu scholar; consequently, it has the same characteristics as the Diwan. With the exception of the information on the reign of King Idris as the ruler of the Bornu kingdom reported by Ibn Battuta, the chain of transmission of information on the Sayfawa rulers can be reconstructed as follows: the genealogy of kings is constructed by scholars and elders and transmitted from one generation of kings to the next, as suggested by the passage contained in the letter of Sultan Uthman b. Idris dating from 1391, 'thus we do register our pedigree as handed down by our Shaykhs '. The letter filed in the royal archives in Cairo was found and published by Al Qalqashandi. It is not known if Al Maqrizi had read that letter or had relied on the work of Al Qalqashandi as both men were leaving and working in the same city at the same time. Both had, however, met scholars and pilgrims from Kanem and Bornu. It can be observed as shown in Table 36 that, while the geneaology of rulers given by Sultan Uthman b. Idris and published by Al Qalqashandi contains four names for kings of the same descent line, that of Al Maqrizi has an additional name from the descent of Da`ud b. Ibrahim. It may be added that the cycles of transmission of this kind of information are much more complex than suggested by the above discussion, as some Kanem and Bornu scholars, on their way to pilgrimage at the Mekka and/or resident at the Madrassa in Cairo may have read these works and included the knowledge gained on the past of their own societies in their interpretation of the history of the Bornu kingdom, and later disseminated it in their teachings.

It clearly appears from the record at hand that the making of genealogies is highly controversial and the events which occured in Kanem and Bornu between c. 1300 and 1400 were subject to conflicting interpretations. The Diwan lists eleven sultans belonging to three descent groups: the annihilated descent group of Sultan Abd Allah (21), that of Sultan Ibrahim (20) which was split into two warring sub-groups, that of Idris (26) and that of Dawud (27) (Table 35). The fragment of genealogy given by Sultan Uthman b. Idris contains only three names from his descent line, specifying that Amr b. Idris, the Martyr, was slain by the Judham Arabs. Finally, the genealogy given by Al Maqrizi contains the names of rulers from two descent lines; he further indicates that during the reign of Uthman b. Idris, before 1397-8, the people from Kanem revolted, apostatized and a Holy War was launched against them. For the same chronological sequence, Al Umari (1301-1349) writing from Cairo and Damascus and using information transmitted to Abd Allah al Saliliji by a Kanembu informant, Uthman al Kanemi, said that both rulers of Al Kanim and Al Barnu had the same formula of correspondence (Levtzion and Hopkins 1981: 277-8), thus suggesting that both kingdoms were equal; an idea shared later by Al Qalqashandi, even though he had not found letters from the king of Kanim: 'I have not found any correspondence of his but it is likely that correspondence from him is similar to correspondence from the ruler of Al Barnu, for he is near to his kingdom.' (Levtzion and Hopkins 1981: 349). For Al Maqrizi, King Al Hadj Ibrahim 'held the throne of Kanim. Kanim is the throne of Barnu', suggesting that Bornu was one of the twelve kingdoms of Kanim (Levtzion and Hopkins 1981: 355). A view similar to that of Al Maqrizi is asserted by Ibn Khaldun, quoting Ibn Said:

In the year 655 A.H./AD 1257 there arrived at Tunis, the Hafsid capital, gifts from the king of Kanim, one of the kings of the Sudan, ruler of Barnu, whose domains lie to the south of Tripoli. Among them was a giraffe, an animal of strange form and incongruous characteristics .(in Levtzion and Hopkins 1981: 337, see also Lange 1982: 318)

As far as the history of the Bornu kingdom is concerned the major problem raised by these different interpretations is that of the development of a new society and the emergence of a new cultural, ethnic and linguistic group which will later be labelled Kanuri. For the Grand Imam Ahmad Furtu, it was Sultan Uthman b. Dawud who had brought about the exodus from Kanem to Kagha in Bornu; for the version of the Diwan referred to here, it is Umar b. Idris who, after taking counsel from the ulema is credited with initiating the move of the Sayfawa to a new land; and finally, for Al Maqrizi, the Kanem wars were a Holy War launched against apostates, who had committedthe most grievous crime in Moslem law.

Chapter 12

State Formation in the Central Sudan

Numerous hypotheses have been presented concerning the development of state formations in Sudanic Africa. Some have already been dismissed as fanciful while others have a better empirical basis (Cuoq 1984, Fisher 1977, 1987, Lange 1977, Mauny 1961, Trimingham 1980), but all of them emphasize one part of the total socio-economic system, and consider it to be the prime mover.

The first group of hypotheses concern what can be termed the 'migration-conquest' theory, and is based on a literal interpretation of the available written record which emphasizes the oriental origin of the first monarchs who succeeded in imposing centralized political systems on native tribes. The so-called Zaghawa dynasty of Duku inferred from the Diwan, which is considered to have resulted from a combination of Berber and Zaghawa tribes, is an example of such a theory, as is the hypothesis of the Yemenite origin of the Sayfawa dynasty (Lange 1977).

The second group of hypotheses emphasizes the role of trans-Saharan trade and the expansion of Islam in the process of state formation. The state apparatus is therefore considered to have been formed in order to secure peace and bureaucratic structures for the sake of trade between North Africa and the <u>Bilad es Sudan</u>. States from the Sudan are thus considered as epiphenomena, mercantilistic in nature (Bovill 1978, Gellner 1977, Hopkins 1980: 20).

It is beyond doubt that migrations, conquests, the development of trans-Saharan trade and the expansion of Islam had a strong impact on Sudanic social formations, and that in some cases they initiated the development of centralized socio-political systems.

However, due to the biases of the written record, the actual dynamics of local systems are poorly understood. New insight into the history of relations between central empires and nomadic tribes in the Middle East in antiquity has shown that direct control of the latter by the former was always temporary. Central monarchs were always looking for a 'gentleman's agreement' with native elites of border areas, mostly through gift exchanges, matrimonial alliances and clientship relations (Briant 1982). By so doing, they secured peace and trade expansion; otherwise, in case of absolute administrative control, the cost of transactions became more and more prohibitive (Blanton 1976). As far as trans-Saharan trade is concerned, the nature of goods included in the transactions was limited by several contraints.

The variety of commodities traded accross the Sahara was limited partly by the length of the journey - the desert part alone taking over six weeks - which meant that highly perishable goods could not be taken, and partly by the high transport charges which are said to have at least doubled the cost of most goods carried and meant that it was worthwhile to carry only things of small bulk and high intrinsic value. (Wickins 1981: 148)

The southward flow of goods therefore consisted of certain foodstuffs, such as dates, wheat, dried grapes and nuts, and, above all, commodities like swords, horses, books, beads of glass, shell or stone, salt, spices, perfumes, manufactures, iron tools, copper, woollen cloths, turbans, aprons and fine enamelware. Slaves, gold, cotton clothes, hides, skins, leather goods, ivory, pepper and kola nuts were the main northward-bound goods (Goody 1980, Hopkins 1980, Mauny 1961, Trimingham 1980: 10-11, Wickins 1981). Gold and slaves were the main goods of the Sahelian zone. The system through which they could be acquired was a complex network, connecting large areas unknown to foreign traders. The traders and political leaders of Sahelian market cities were obliged to deal with middlemen, and the middlemen were mostly members of local elites. The slave trade, for example, often involved warfare and raiding, and many scholars (Hopkins 1980, Thornton 1982, Wickins 1981: 164-165) agree that African middlemen were controlled the landward side of the trade. The same argument applies to gold in West Africa, where gold-fields were always located in the marshes of centralized states. According to Bathily (1977: 114-15), great empires did not take control over gold production per se. In fact, they only had control over the trade, while production always stayed beyond the reach of great emperors. While explaining the nature of the gold trade, Bovill (1978: 79-85) expressed the same idea:

The merchants once tried to discover the source of the gold by treacherously capturing one of the timid negroes. He pined to death without saying a word, and it was three years before the negroes would resume the trade, and then only because they had no other way of satisfying their craving for salt. (Bovill 1978: 82)

If, as suggested by the above discussion, local social systems were at least partially involved in the trans-Saharan trade, they had probably witnessed some in-depth transformations; these changes may have been qualitative and quantitative. Qualitative changes may have concerned the rise and fall of families, groups and clans, the achievement of new and prestigious statuses; while quantitative ones may have concerned the increased size of domestic groups, the number of clients and dependants, and the pooling of labour force and military power. In this perspective, local households were fully involved in the process of state formation as demonstrated by Warnier (1983: 596, my translation) in his sociological analysis of Pre-colonial Bamenda:

everywhere on the plateau, the household was the primary unit of production and consumption. These households varied in size. ...But in all of them kinship assumes the role of relations of production. It determines who may have access to resources and means of production, it organizes the process of production and the distribution of goods and services.

The households were differentially integrated into the inter-regional trade network, directly or via the village and/or chiefdom levels. Their dynamic interactions in time and space were probably the major factors in the rise and fall of paramount chiefdoms on the Bamenda plateau. These observations shed new light on the mechanism of trade in ancient societies and its interaction with social systems.

State Formation: Definitions, Theory and Method

The process of state formation is multi-faceted and includes both qualitative and quantitative transformations of human social systems. The implications are economic, political, religious, demographic and environmental. To grasp the complexity involved in this set of multiple interacting components, we need some clearly stated definitions, a theory which links the different components and a method which makes it possible to fit factual evidence together.

Definitions

The concept of state formation refers to the study of a process of social change from a former social stage A to a latter social stage B. At this point in our discussion two major categories of state formation can be singled out: the first is the category of primary or pristine state formation in which particular societies experience internal processes of transformation leading to the development of new and centralized socio-political organizational features. The second, characterized as secondary state formation, concerns cases of the development of centralized political systems following influence or pressure from neighbouring or alien societies. Depending on the category, therefore, the processes of state formation may require a great deal of time or be relatively sudden. Whatever the case however, the opportunities to observe this process ethnographically are very rare and the implications of such observations are often limited in scope. When available, the ethno-historical record may give some clues if researchers succeed in devising adequate techniques of interpretation (Conrad and Demarest 1984, Holl 1985, 1993b, Vansina 1990, Wright 1986, Yoffee and Cowgill 1988).

There is a huge amount of literature on the problem of the development of state formation (Blanton et al. 1981, Cahiers d'études africaines Special Issue 1982, Chapman 1990, Claessen 1984, Claessen and Van de Velde 1987, Eisenstadt et al. 1983, 1988, Fortes and Evans-Pritchard 1940, Friedman and Rowlands 1977, Haas 1982, Johnson 1976, 1987, Jones and Kautz 1981, Levy and Holl 1988, Quilter and Stocker 1983, Steward 1955, Wittfogel 1977, Wright 1977, Wright and Johnson 1975, etc.). In their now classic book on African political systems, Fortes and Evans-Pritchard (1940) presented two main types of political organization of African societies: the segmentary system and the centralized one. They stated that: 'those who consider that a state should be defined by the presence of governmental institutions will regard the first group as stateless societies and the second group as primitive states' (1940: 5), and the transformation from the first type to the second was briefly explained explained in terms of invasion or conquest (1940: 10). It is now clear that the situation is not so simple, and according to Alexandre (1982: 229) relations between stateless societies and centralized ones can no longer be based upon arguments of mutual exclusiveness.

Attempts at a universally acceptable definition of the state are doomed to failure because of the multiple facets of the phenomenon. The numerous definitions already used by various scholars merely need to be operationalized; in other words, we need to give them an empirical content and visibility. Following Haas (1982: 3), a state can be defined 'initially in the most general terms as a society in which there is a centralized and specialized institution of government'; the stage just below state level will therefore show trends towards centralization and specialization. These socio-political organizations have been granted various names in the anthropological and historical literature: chiefdoms, pristine or 'asiatic' states, statelets or segmentary states.

According to Carneiro (1981: 45), a chiefdom is an autonomous political unit comprising a number of villages or communities under the permanent control of a paramount chief. He considers chiefdoms to be the only route to the primary state; their emergence was therefore a qualitative step, and everything that followed, including the rise of states and empires, was in a sense merely quantitative. Pristine or 'asiatic' states emerged from the tribal system (Friedman and Rowlands 1977: 216-20); this concept is explicitly restricted to the earliest state formations. The size of the 'asiatic' state may not exceed an area of 20-30 km radius with a population of around 10,000. The size of this political unit may depend largely on the ability to centralize the economy and to prevent accumulation of labour and surplus in peripheral areas.

Riley, quoted by Doolittle (1984: 13) characterizes statelets as possessing ranked rather than egalitarian societies with a ruling class, economic life being based on irrigation agriculture and heavily oriented toward trade.

In his discussion on the Alur system and political theory, Southall (1970: 246-7) stated that:

'the distinction between state and segmentary organisation is theoretically valid, and at abstract level intermediate forms demand no separate category. But in any scheme of classification which claims empirical relevance, the criteria of legitimate isolation are different and any empirical form which has a certain frequency, stability and structural consistency must receive due consideration.

Hence, he called this intermediate form a segmentary state, which is a political system combining localized lineage segmentation with specialized political institutions, while trying to trace its development from the interaction of contrasting social structures, and pointing out its implications for the theory of state formation.

From the selected sample of definitions of early states presented above, it is clear that there are major lines of agreement between the different scholars quoted. Whatever the main emphasis of each of them, the chiefdom, the pristine or 'asiatic' state, the statelet and the segmentary state all appear to be supra-communities and regional phenomena, which have spatial correlates in the form of settlement patterns accessible to archaeological investigations (Blanton et al. 1979). Transformations in other spheres of social activity are also implied. Social stratification, labour and production intensification and exchanges, ideologies of political legitimation, demography and environmental conditions interact to produce new patterns.

Theory

To avoid the 'prime-mover' bias, a systemic approach is needed to analyse the problem of state formation in the Central Sudan (Bisson 1982, Butzer 1981, Eisenstadt et al. 1983, 1988, Phillipson 1979). In general terms, the problems dealt with in this chapter can be stated as those of scale, integration and complexity, or, from another point of view, structure, system and dialectics (Blanton et al. 1981, Godelier 1977, 1980, Kowalewski et al. 1983).

Scale refers to size of the unit being analysed; this unit may be a spatial one, for instance, a region, a site, a compound, a house floor, a piece of written historical source, its words, its syntax, its organization. It may also be a social unit, a household, a village community, a clan, a confederation of clans, a dynasty, or any other kind of aggregate of people. Thus scale may vary according to the analytical level of investigation.

Integration refers to the dynamic relations between units - their interdependence - which may be conceptualized as a system-wide regulation of information flow. This integration may be of several kinds - economic, political, social, religious, etc. 'Depending on the kind of component units, the connections are established as flow of material, energy, information or people. The greater the flow through interconnecting channels, the greater the interdependence' (Blanton et al. 1981: 20).

Complexity refers to the extent to which there is functional differentiation among societal units, and is therefore obviously connected to integration. Theoretically, complexity can be partitioned into two main components; horizontal and vertical differentiation. The former refers to functional specialization among parts of equivalent rank, and the latter to a hierarchy of functionally diverse parts of a social system However, according to Blanton et al. (1981: 231):

it may seem that by this discussion we have unnecessarily complicated the issue of state origins. But on examination our statements concerning the concepts of vertical and horizontal differentiation, integration, and scale are much less astract and much more operational than the key concepts of many of the current hypotheses of state origins.

Hence whatever evolutionary model one assumes, it is almost obvious that the process of state formation implies increasing scales of inclusiveness in every sphere of human experience. A discussion of some components of societal activities - political, economic, and ideological factors - will show the analytical potentials of the Blanton et al. scheme.

Concerning political factors, causal explanations of increasing political control in human societies are commonly made on the basis of a division between 'conflict theories' and 'integrative theories' (Haas 1981, 1982). From the point of view of 'conflict theories', the acquisition of political power by a social group is through the control of critical resources; thus this group is in position to enforce obedience and manipulate power for its benefit. On the other hand, 'integrative theories' emphasize coordination of different social components to minimize the cost of decisions for the benefit of the whole society. This distinction is better illustrated by the debate in anthropology over the process implied in social hierarchy, social stratification, or, in the terms used in this study, vertical differentiation. Discussions of the Indian caste system led to the emergence of two traditions of explanations: the ritualists and the power theorists.

According to Dumont (1966, 1977, 1983), one of the major proponents of the ritualist position, the underlying logic of the Indian caste system is the opposition between the pure and the impure ; thus, as one moves from the top to the bottom of the social hierarchy, purity decreases. The position of individuals in relation to each other is defined accordingly, and power, forced to express itself in religious terms is asserted to be under the dominance of values, that is, religion or status. 'Political theory persists in identifying itself with a theory of power, that is, in considering a minor problem as a fundamental one, which is contained by the relations between "power" and values or ideology' (Dumont 1977: 19).

The power theorists (see Borgström 1977: 327) consider caste as directly comparable to other forms of social stratification. It is therefore only an instance of a more general phenomenon, based on peculiar rules of recruitment and interaction that are not ordained by values but are defined by the ruling strata in the society; hence status is secondary to power. Some Marxist scholars share this point of view (Kubbel in Gellner 1977).

According to Borgström (1977: 325) these extreme positions both fail to explain how power is related to value in the Indian caste systemean After all, both claim to say something about the same institution, the caste system, and if both are really necessary to understand that phenomenon, this must mean that they are situational and should be referable to a common basis that accounts for both. In general terms, social stratification refers to all forms of social inequality and may include caste and rigid occupation classes as well as age and sex stratification. Narrowly defined, it may only deal with specific kinds of inequality in which society-wide strata are obviously recognized. Social stratification is thus a basic element of social organization in all human and some animal societies; 'interpersonal and intergroup relations of dominance and submission, rank or hierarchy appear wherever people live together' (Cancian 1976: 227).

For our purpose, social stratification is better explained in terms of responses to changes of scale in a society's decision-making process (Johnson 1982). In situations where sufficient numbers of people accumulate and have to share the same space, considerin the finite capacity of the human brain to acquire, process and store information, and the inability of humans to be at more than one place at the same time, the social creation of differentiation occurs. It therefore appears that, in varying proportions, conflict versus integrative and status versus power rationales may be present at the same time within any socio-political context, mainly because the origin of a specific political condition may have little or nothing to do with the perceptions of those being ruled (Jones and Kautz 1981: 20).

Discussion of economic factors implied in the emergence of state organization is often made at the macro level of trade, external communication and environmental complementarity. The importance of this macro level cannot be ignored; however, analysis on this scale tends to under-emphasize the contribution of lower level economic components such as households. If economy is defined as a sphere of social activities dealing with the procurement of resources and their distribution and consumption for the maintenance and the reproduction of the society as a whole, in many cases the household appears to be the primary socio-economic entity which is horizontally and/or vertically differentiated. One of the critical features of the household economy or domestic mode of production (Sahlins 1968, 1976) is the recruitment of labour. In self-sustaining societies, the forces of production are essentially land, livestock and tools. They are relatively easily accessible to all members of the social group, but the skills necessary to perform various socio economic tasks 'provide those who possess them with genuine authority over the laymen since the continuation of the group depends on this knowledge' (Meillassoux 1980: 137). This knowledge is often acquired with seniority, supporting the fundamental senior/junior relationships. Considering the overlapping nature of generational structure in all societies, one may agree that there are always at least three generations present in a living society: the old, the middle-aged and the young.

Societies need some mechanism which allows individuals to give to the old and have confidence that they in turn will be the recipients of gifts when they are old. Money, ritual knowledge, clubs, land, kinship groups, and a host of others are all social arrangements which help to inspire this confidence and to achieve an optimal allocation of consumption. (Walsh 1983: 647)

In this perspective, kinship relations in a household are simultaneously relations of production, and two types of circulation of goods and services can be inferred. The seniors receive the juniors' prestations and then supervise the whole group output. Delayed reciprocity is the normal system of generational devolution of the cycle of prestation/redistribution implied by kinship status. A successful household head may therefore have a large number of dependants, wives, children and clients, in order to secure its labour force, a large amount of output, and its authority and prestige. The qualitative link between the household structure and the community level is based upon these features. In the anthropological literature, surplus production is sometimes considered to be the key variable in vertical social differentiation. In a review of theories of social stratification in sociology and anthropology, Cancian (1976: 230-1) persuasively argued that the idea that stratification resulted from the creation of a material surplus is not only a simplistic view, but also has little support since its definition in absolute terms is not workable. However, considered in relative terms, the concept of surplus may be useful as an indication of increased production beyond the subsistence requirements of a specific production unit. Economic differentiation based on control of people is not operative in terms of so-called 'surplus' production but only in terms of prestige arising from a large compound (Bohannan and Bohannan 1968: 223). Coupled with the acquisition of prestige goods, a high food-output strengthens the position of a household head as a potential community leader. Prestige goods may often be of exotic raw materials, shell, stone, or other socially valued matter (iron, silver, gold, etc.); they may also be in livestock - cattle, horses or camels, for instance. Whatever the case, prestige goods are not only valued on a material basis, but, belonging to the higher level of the exchange hierarchy, their social value is predominant. They are insignia of wealth and success (Itéanu 1983, Mauss 1990). It is thus possible for an individual to invest wealth if he 'converts up' into a morally superior category; to convert subsistence wealth into prestige wealth and both into women is the 'economic aim of individual Tiv, such conversion is the ultimate type of maximization' (Bohannan and Bohannan 1968: 234-5).

If the dynamics of the household economy are correlated to the sphere of prestige goods exchange, it may be one possible way to increase vertical differentiation in a community. A successful household head with a large following and a large amount of output who converts his wealth into prestige items may become, on the 'big-man' model, a man of prestige and gain authority over his fellows at the community level and beyond.

The place of ideological factors in the process of state formation is probably the most important even if they are the most difficult to grasp (Conrad and Demarest 1984). Ideological systems convey meanings to facts of life and are instrumental in competition for legitimacy between potential rulers. Working on African data, Eisenstadt et al. (1983: 12-37, 1988: 19-25) found that the emergence of states in Africa is not only the result of structural differentiation of political roles, but is also strongly correlated to symbolic differentiation of the political sphere through its concrete manifestations in different types of centres. That is, according to the fusion or separation of secular and religious offices, or their various combinations, the forms of emergent states are different. There are, consequently, congruent societies in which the articulation of the elite functions is fitted into the organizational specialization of the social division of labour, and non-congruent systems 'manifest in the crystallization of distinct articulators of existing kin-based models of cultural order in societies that had undergone processes of task specialization' (Eisenstadt et al. 1988: 23).

In the absence of naked coercive force, religious sanctions provided a path toward the development of political centralisation. ... The amount of resources both human and natural, expended on religion in the form of temple construction and tribute must have had a profound effect on the configuration of early state economies as well as on the forms of political organization developed to organize and direct the exploitation of these resources. (Keatinge 1981: 187)

Method and Expectations

This short discussion on some of the factors involved in the formation of states does not aim to review research on the origin of states (Claessen and Van de Velde: 1987, Wright 1986). Trans-Saharan trade, Islam, domestic susbsistence strategies, diversity of socio-economic systems, interaction between different ethnic groups and varying strategies of alliance and competition all shaped the social systems of the Central Sudan during the last millennium The Diwan is an important window on the past but it can not take us very far in the understanding of the peculiar evolution of the past societies of our study area if considered in isolation. As far as Central Sudan is concerned, we need to integrate all the data available on the past of that area: archaeological data may be helpful in clarifying part of the history of settlement in the study area in relation to changes in the environment.

Unfortunately, archaeological research carried out in Kanem and Bornu during recent decades was not explicitly geared to study the problem of the emergence of state formation. The difference in size of sites and data on regional settlement hierarchy are the best indications of the development of centralized socio-political system. Central settlements such as Birni Ghazzargamo, the capital of the Bornu Kingdom from c. 1450-1820 were generally the largest in the region and were characterized by particular features such as earthenwalls surrounding the city, a royal palace and elites' residences built with fire-hardened bricks and situated at the centre of gravity of the community space. District centres were often smaller in size and controlled a varying number of villages and hamlets located in the 'countryside'. In the southern part of the Chad basin, in the clay plain stretching from Nigeria in the west to northern Cameroon and Chad Republic in the east, there is evidence of walled settlements which emerged between c.

1000-1500 (Holl 1987, 1988b), surrounded by smaller mounds of former villages, hamlets and seasonal camps. The area covered by such small polities varied from 7-10 km in radius. Theoretically, it was such early small polities of Chadic speakers located along the Yobe River on the western shore of Lake Chad and generically termed 'Soo' (Lange 1987) who were allied with the early proto-Kanuri speakers, and probably were slowly conquered and assimilated to become the Kanuri. Evidence of long-distance trade in prestige goods such as carnelian beads from the Adrar-n-Ifogha and the Tilemsi valley in modern Mali (Gaussen and Gaussen 1989), copper and brass artefacts from Takkeda and Marandet in the Aïr region in the modern Niger Republic (Grébénart 1985, Bernus and Cressier 1991) have been found from archaeological contexts dating from c. 850 at Daïma (Connah 1981), Mdaga (Lebeuf et al. 1980), Sou Blamé Radjill (Rapp 1984) and Houlouf (Holl 1988a). It is thus argued that there may have been strong competition between peer-polities of the Chadian plain at the end of the first and beginning of the second millennium (Renfrew and Cherry 1986), were they proto-Kanuri, proto-Bulala or Chadic. According to the Diwan, after a series of military setbacks against the Chadic speakers (the Soo) and the Bulala, the Kanuri, then termed 'the Believers or Moslems' in the Chronicle of Imam Ahmad Furtu (Lange 1987), had finally succeeded in overwhelming all their competitors by 1600.

Following Wright (1986: 357-8), it therefore appears that, in the Central Sudan as well as in many other areas which had witnessed the formation of state societies, (1) pre-state societies with two to three levels of control hierarchy persisted for centuries, with intense competition and much replacement of centres and no doubt of paramounts, but with little or no increase in socio-political complexity; (2) state emergence occurs in limited areas with dense concentrations of similar-sized centres, often with populations dispersed and reduced as a result of long-term competition and increasing overt conflict; (3) correlated with the emergence of three- to four-level central control hierarchies, rapid population nucleation occurs, probably at the expense of the defeated or threatened neighbours; (4) Coincident with these changes, the intensity of conflict increases, and in some cases there is documentary evidence that raiding is replaced by organized warfare with the conquest and reorganization of surrounding areas. These different expectations from our model of state formation will be evaluated in the light of the available archaeological, palaeoclimatic and historical linguistic data.

Chapter 13

Archaeological, Palaeoclimatic and Linguistic Background to the History of Kanem-Bornu

Archaeological, palaeoclimatic and historical linguistic research can provide additional information on the early history of Central Sudan. However, to be really useful they have to be considered critcally. Each field of research has its own problems and methods which are not as homegeneous as may be thought from a simple outsider position. To take but one example, the dating of an archaeological context, the radiocarbon technique is based on a complex series of manipulations starting with the selection of an adequate sample of material, followed by laboratory work and ending with a discussion of reliability in terms of probability range of the figures given by the laboratory and the translation into calendar years. In this regard, and to avoid the false precision of neat figures, ranges of double sigma (i.e. double standard deviation always given with radiocarbon dates in the form +/- 100, for example) which increases the probability for a given date to be exact to 95 per cent, is used in this study for uncalibrated dates of tested archaeological sites.

Archaeological Research in Kanem and Bornu

Archaeological research is still in its infancy in our study area. However, during the last three decades notable progress has been made both in Kanem and Bornu, even if the number of excavated and dated sites, which amounts to twelve, is as yet too low to allow the reconstruction of an accurate picture of the history of human settlements.

Nonetheless, the results of both archaeological surveys and excavations accomplished so far provide an important contribution to the debate on the early history of the southern Central Sudan societies (Bivar and Shinnie 1962, Connah 1969a, b, 1971, 1981, 1984, Coppens 1969, Holl 1987, Lebeuf et al. 1980, Treinen-Claustre 1978, 1982). There are some specific problems for archaeological fieldwork in Africa which are very important but are beyond the scope of the present study; it will be enough to specify that the size of our usual test excavations is often very small relative to the size of studied settlements; this means that the dating of sites and the reconstruction of settlements' histories are always opened to further revision and improvement.

In Kanem, archaeological surveys and excavations, framed in cultural-historical terms, were focused on the eastern part of the region, in the surroundings of the city of Koro Toro. Consequently, nothing is known of the distribution of archaeological sites in that part of Kanem situated on the eastern shore of the Lake Chad which is of more direct interest for the research problem under discussion in this volume. Treinen-Claustre (1978, 1982) has mapped 127 sites in eastern Kanem, dating from the Late Stone Age - or Neolithic - to the Late Iron Age. Nine sites were tested and dated, the samples of radiocarbon dates obtained ranging from 610-210 bc (uncalibrated dates) for the settlement of Kebir Bosa, to 1140-1500 ad from Bahali I (Table 36). Late Stone Age sites dating between c. 2000 and 500 bc, are relatively sparse and confined to the 300-320 m contour line of the Early Holocene Megachad (Figure 11).

Early Iron Age sites datiing from c. 400 bc to 500 ad, are much more numerous and are characterized by the presence of 'Grooved Ware' attested in about 60 sites out of 127. Iron implements, mostly items of personal adornment and weapons, are present but rare, and no smelting installation was found. The majority of sites are relatively small scatters of potsherds and other artefacts, varying in size from 10-100 m in diameter, thus suggesting that these locales were probably used as seasonal and temporary camps. However, one important settlement, termed Site 7 (16° 04' N. lat./ 18° 27' E. long.), covering a surface of 4 hectares was discovered near Koro Toro. It contains evidence of 21 circular huts disposed in concentric circles around a central space. Eighteen of the huts discovered have diameters varying from 3.5-6 m and three have diameters varying from 10-12 m and were built with poles and straw (Treinen-Claustre 1982: 176). Three important cemeteries with barrows, having respectively 400, 80 and 100 burials were found at Nemra I (16° 18' N. lat./ 18° 33' E. long.), Nemra II (16° 18' N. lat./ 18° 31' E. long.) and Donsanas (15° 38' N. lat. 18° 34' E. long.). Hunting, fishing and the gathering of landsnails and freshwater molluscs seem to have been the major components of the subsistence systems. No positive evidence pertaining to the practice of livestock husbandry and agriculture has been found. The pattern of settlements of Early Iron Age societies of the Koro Toro area seems to have had two basic components: relatively important and stable sites, dwelling and burial sites, complemented by series of seasonal and temporary camps.

The middle sequence, partially overlapping with the previous one, has been termed 'Haddad Culture' (Coppens 1969) or the 'Culture of Koro Toro' (Treinen-Claustre 1978, 1982). This archaeological culture is characterized by the presence of finely made wares, often painted in black and red and decorated with geometric motifs which are claimed to have been introduced from Upper Egypt and Nubia, and the massive presence of iron smelting features (Figure 12). It appears that this period, dating from c. 200-1200 AD witnessed the emergence of craft specialization, with localized groups of blacksmiths and potters, and the development large and permanent settlements divided into iron smelting sites with numerous furnaces and enormous slag heaps, and dwelling sites (Table 36). The people from the Koro Toro Culture settled on mounds with surface extent varying from 0.5-10 hectares, as is the case at Bochianga, some of them being as high as 10 mean Most of the settlements are now located between the 240 m and 280 m contour lines and their density is the highest of the archaeological sequence of the whole area. The categories of artefacts are much more diverse, comprising zoomorphic and anthropomorphic figurines, grinding equipment and various iron implements including hoe blades and axes. Exotic materials such as carnelian beads are also attested. The subsistence system is also more complex and diversified, comprising agriculture, cattle husbandry and occasionally bones of sheep/goats. These activities of food-production were complemented by fishing, hunting and gathering from the wild, and storage features have been uncovered in almost all the surveyed and tested settlements. The Koro Toro Culture is considered as the climactic phase of the whole proto-historic sequence of settlement in eastern Kanem, which was followed by a period of decline in terms of decreased density of settlements, impoverished material culture and lower quantities of archaeological evidence on sites.

The presence of a Later Iron Age sequence is very poorly attested as the density of the population had sharply decreased, probably due to the worsening climatic conditions; it is tentatively dated from the twelfth to the fifteenth century, as suggested by a radiocarbon date from the site of Bahali I (Treinen-Claustre 1982: 181). This is an extensive and shallow surface site with five distinct clusters of archaeological evidence; small terracotta figurines have been uncovered with pieces of an arm-ring in alloyed copper and few glass beads.

From this short archaeological summary, it appears that at the crisis period of the Sayfawa rulers, from 1200-1400 AD, there was a major shift in the distribution of population in eastern Kanem, probably due to adverse climatic conditions. It may be suggested, as will be shown later, that in the process of reorganization of the settlement location system thus initiated, people were preferentially looking for wetter lands, like the shores of Lake Chad, the Bahr el Ghazzal, the Shari, the Yedseram, the El Beid and the Yobe rivers. In other words, the changing patterns in the distribution of human settlements during the Later Iron Age may have resulted in a scramble for watered areas, and a correlated competition for new lands between different social groups and formations.

Archaeological research conducted in northern Bornu, the heartland of the Bornu kingdom, was framed in adaptive terms in order to study the relationships between Man and his environment (Connah 1969a, b, 1971, 1981, 1984, 1985). In his sudies on the settlements of the Yobe flood-plain, Connah has mapped thirteen sites divided into two variants: two flat sites, Birni Ghazzargamo, the former capital of the kingdom of Bornu and Gambaru; and eleven Yobe-type mounds: Ajere, Bargaram, Bagada, Daia, Duguri, Gashagar, Juballam, Lowan Gajiri Dunes, Ngauro Kura, North Duguri and Yau (Figure 11).

The gap in the distribution of archaeological sites in the middle Yobe is very probably only an artefact of fieldwork logistics; the area was flooded at the time of my survey. Certainly the high-level air-photographic cover that was available of the Yobe area in the mid 1960s showed more sites than have yet been located. (Connah 1981: 200)

One flat site (Birni Ghazzargamo) and two Yobe-type mounds (Yau: Mound 3 and Ajere) have been selected for test excavations and pottery, mostly potsherds, are the most abundant category of material remains collected. The thickness of archaeological stratigraphy varies from 7.75 m (21 feet) at Yau, Shaft A, to 3.20 m (9 feet) at Ajere with 4.30 m (13 feet) at Birni Ghazzargamo. The archaeological material was recorded and collected following artificial stratigraphic units (a spit), measuring one foot (about 0.30 cm, Table 37). Following that recording system, there are twenty-one spits at Yau:

Shaft A, thirteen at Birni Ghazzargamo: Cutting I, and nine at Ajere (Table 38). As emphasized by Connah (1981), the distribution of archaeological records throughout the stratigraphy seems to occur in patterned variations.

The quantity of sherds and animal bones fluctuated as if indicating peaks of settlement activity. The cultural material other than pottery also showed similar variations which to some degree were in stratigraphic positions comparable with those of the sherds and bones. Although spit volumes varied greatly and the shafts tapered with increasing depth, these do appear to have been real variations in the quantity of cultural material deposited at diffrent times. (Connah 1981: 204)

Following the idea suggested in the above quote, it may be informative to attempt to translate the archaeological stratigraphies recorded into more relevant cultural units related as closely as possible to occupation episodes. It appears that there are nine episodes of occupation at Yau, and four at Birnin Gazargamo and Ajere (Table 38).
The archaeological site of Yau, located at a distance of some 21 km from the shore of lake Chad is a large complex of nine, and possibly eleven mounds; the biggest and the highest, referred to as Mound 3 was selected for excavation. It is a crescent-shaped mound measuring approximately 150 m long and 65 m wide, roughly oriented East/West. At Yau, Mound 3, as well as at Ajere, the archaeological 'deposits consisted of a mixture of sand and ash with a varying charcoal content, deposited in layers and lenses of darker or lighter material which were sometimes finely banded' (Connah 1981: 203-4). The distribution of collected cultural material is bi-modal, with one peak during the third occupation (spits 15-17) and a second one during occupation 8 (spits 4-5) (Figure 13). Occupation 1 (spits 20-1) at a depth of 7.00-7.75 m, is dated to 780-1140 (Table 39); occupation 3, tentatively dated with a charcoal sample collected from the top fill of feature 5 at a depth of 4.90 m, had occurred in 750-1110; occupation 5 (spits 10-12) is dated to 740-1180 from a sample collected in spit 11 at a depth of 3.70-4.00 m and, finally, occupation 8 occurred in 1055-1495, dated from a sample collected in spit 4 at a depth of 0.80-1.20 mean The later deposit of occupation 1 which may span to 1500-1600 has not been directly dated.
At Birni Ghazzargamo, situated near the upper Yobe River, three test excavations were carried out; cuttings I and II on a small mound located in the south of the palace site,

114

and cutting III within the remains of the palace. The settlement is very large with many architectural complexes (Figure 14).

It consists of an enormous earth rampart enclosing a rough circle. This rampart still stands about 7 metres high and the distance across the enclosure is about 2 kilometres. There are five entrances. Traces of ditch - (in fact a quarry ditch, from which the material for the rampart must have been dug. ... (Connah 1981: 229) - can be seen in few places along the outside of the rampart and it is likely that originally it ran the whole way along but is now silted up. Inside this vast enclosure are a number of red brick ruins consisting of a large complex in the centre and a number of other smaller buildings scattered throughout the enclosed area. (Bivar and Shinnie 1962: 3)

The site stratigraphy seems to have been disturbed by intensive burrowing and insects' activities; however, the pattern which emerges is that of increasing settlement activity from occupations 1-4, as measured by the quantity of discarded cultural material (Table 38, Figure 13). Occupations 2 and 3 are dated to 1410-1830 from a composite sample of charcoal collected in spits 5, 7 and 8, at depths varying from 1.40 to 2.70 m. This date is congruent with the historical record on the foundation of the capital of the Bornu kingdom; but it is worth noting that there is one earlier occupation episode, with a deposit 1.60 m thick which was not dated with radiocarbon because of the absence of any adequate sample. The settlement may thus be much older than claimed and may have become the capital city of Sayfawa later. Evidence of fired bricks and clay had been found in cuttings II and III, and all of these were retrieved in occupations 3 and 4 deposits, suggesting that they were introduced to the site later.

Ajere is a complex of four mounds located some 3 km from the shores of Lake Chad, in a sand-dunes context. The archaeological deposits were so loose that it has been impossible with the available field equipment to proceed with the excavation down to the bottom levels; the site has thus been tested down to a depth of 3.20 m, representing only the upper half of the Ajere archaeological sequence (Connah 1981: 212-13). No radiocarbon date is available for Ajere, but according to the researcher, the pottery would suggest a date later than Yau for the upper archaeological sequence. The distribution of cultural material shows that settlement activity was relatively intense at the bottom of the excavation unit which is here termed occupation 1, followed by a sharp decrease in occupations 2 and 3, and was then on the rise again in occupation 4

(Table 38, Figure 13). In this regard, the Ajere sequence may have been contemporaneous with ccupations 8 and 9 of Yau, followed by that of Birni Ghazzargamo (Tables 39 and 40).

The variations of the recorded cultural material extensively discussed by the author of the research, and presented in abridged form in Table 41 will not be repeated here. It will be enough to say that they attest the existence of a specific cultural entity which had settled in the Yobe flood plain as early as the eighth century (Figure 15) The subsistence system was composed of cattle and sheep/goats husbandry and the cultivation of millet, complemented by fishing for large fish such as Lates niloticus - the Nile perch - and Synodontis sp. probably caught from the Yau river; hunting of wildfowl and some mammals which have not been identified, and the gathering of freshwater molluscs. Iron metallurgy is attested in all settlements by weapons, slag as well as crucibles and tuyères; spindle-whorls, suggesting the practice of weaving, have also been found; but there is no exotic material be it alloyed copper or carnelian beads which are numerous in settlements from the clay plain in the south. Keeping in mind the limited sample of tested settlements, the Yobe area seems to have been relatively isolated from the inter-regional exchange network which was active in the south.

The differences between the material record from the Yobe sandy area and that of the clay plains - Firki - from the south and southwest is so neat that there is enough supporting ground for the idea of the development of early Kanuri settlements in northern Bornu (Connah 1981, Connah and Freeth 1989, Holl 1987, 1988a, b, 1990, 1992, A.M.D. Lebeuf 1992, J.P. Lebeuf 1992, Lebeuf et al. 1980). There is however an important gap in the geographic coverage of archaeological investigations between eastern Kanem, with its recorded past cultural sequences dating from the Late Stone Age to c. 1500 AD (Coppens 1969, Treinen-Claustre 1978, 1982), and the Yobe valley area which has been settled from c. 750 AD (Table 39, Figure 15). The settlement of groups of Kanembu herders and fishermen in the Yobe area probably resulted from large-scale redistribution of population which lasted for centuries between the eastern and western shores of Lake Chad and the neighbouring river valleys.

Palaeoclimatology of the last Millennium

Palaeoecological studies have shown that Lake Chad had experienced major fluctuations in prehistoric, historic as well as present times (Blench 1991, Grove 1985, Maley 1973, 1981, Maley and Seignobos 1989, Nicholson 1980, Servant and Servant-

Vildary 1971, 1980). The observed fluctuations bear on the depth and the surface area of the lake; in order to assess the consequences of these variations for human settlements, it is important to consider different time scales: seasonal variations within the same year, 10, 100, 1,000 and multi-millennial cycles (Figure 16). On average, the present-day level of Lake Chad varies from 282 m above sea level in good years, to 280 m above sea level in drought years, during which it is almost dry. Theoretically, in normal years, at peaks of flood in November / December, water collected from the whole drainage basin and rainfall is extensively distributed in a single and coherent lake which is later divided, at the peaks of dry seasons in March / April, into distinct water sheets depending on the depths of lake floor, one centred on the Yobe River in the north and the other centered on the Chari in the south. In drought years, free water is confined to the south and the northern part of the lake situated beyond 13° N. latitude is bare and dry.(Figure 17). During such drought periods there are radical changes in the distribution of population and their economic and subsistence activities. Such a radical change has recently been studied (Blench 1991) and deserves to be considered in more detail, as it may shed some light on the processes which may have generated some important historical phenomena, such as the migration of some groups of Kanembu speakers in the Yobe area.

In 1990, Lake Chad has virtually disappeared and was replaced by open plains of swampy grassland and even dry savannah. There was a dry-season road from Baga in Nigeria to Baga Sola in Chad Republic across the centre of the lake. 'The most notable effect is the creation of extensive new region of pasture. The former flooding regime covered most of the grasslands during the period of high water, leaving only tumuli which were the encampments of the Yedina people' (Blench 1991: 1). The Yedina, with their large-horned Kuri cattle, which could swim from island to island as the water rose, are well adapted to the lake environment. With the desiccation of the lake, this advantage of the Yedina is lost and they now face intensive competition for resources with other ethnic groups.

> Now that much of the lake no longer floods, the challenge from biting flies is much reduced, which has attracted pastoralists from a wide area of the Sahel. The Kuri no longer has a comparative advantage and most of the incomers are FulBe with zebu cattle especially Rahadji, Bunaji and Sokoto Gudali breeds. In addition, there are Kanembu (Sugurti and Kuburi), Kanuri-related groups such as the Koyam and the various groups of Shuwa Arabs.

In addition, camel-herders such as the Uled Suliman are using the lake-floor in the dry season'. (Blench 1991: 1)

Additionally, cultivators producing tomatoes, onions, waterleaf, peppers, etc. for sale in cities, are also attracted by the fertile lands. The density of occupation is so low that their gardens are not threatened by livestock which does not need to be under tight control.'The consequence is that the aerial survey recorded some of the highest densities of livestock ever recorded in Africa. At peak periods there may be as many as half-a-million cattle in the area marked as open water on conventional maps' (Blench 1991: 2). According to Yaqut writing in 1224, the wealth of the king of the Kanim (Zaghawa) consists of livestock such as sheep, cattle, camels and horses. The greater part of the crop of their country being sorghum and cowpeas and then wheat. The means of subsistence of the Kanim is crops and the ownership of livestock. (in Levtzion and Hopkins 1981: 171). It can there be hypothesized that, during drought years the Kanim may have taken advantage of the new opportunities offered by the desiccation of Lake Chad, an expansion which may have been countered and resisted by the usual dwellers of Lake Chad, the Saw.

The curve of fluctuations in the water level of Lake Chad during the last millennium has been established through combined efforts of geologists and palynologists (Figure 18). These results have been achieved through the analysis of various sediment samples collected from different stations situated on the shores and within the lake (Figure 11 C). The lake level was relatively high during two periods, in c. 1000-1200 and c. 1600-1700. In c. 1250-1300, the level of the lake decreases to 283 m above sea level .and then rises to 284 m above sea level between c. 1300 and 1400. For almost one and half or even two centuries, between c. 1400 and 1600, with a minor fluctuation, the lake seems to have virtually disappeared. After c. 1700, there is a regular pattern of succession of three very low and three moderately high lake levels, congruent with the three sets of famines recorded in the Diwan (Table 42, Figure 19). As shown in Table 42 radiocarbon dates from samples collected from the southern shore of the lake in the Chari delta, Bol Berim and Bol Tandal from the Kanem shore, Nioum in Kanem, Kouka in the Bahr el Ghazzal and Foga in Mangari in Niger Republic support the existence of a low lake level between c. 1395 and 1460 or 1500. The sample from Bosso in the Yobe area support the existence of another low lake level period in c. 1790 or 1830. And finally, the samples from Ngouri and Nedeley in the Bahr el Ghazzal and Karagou in Mangari support the existence of a high lake level in c. 1615-1670.

A Short Excursus in Historical Linguistics

Kanuri is a language from the Kanembu-Kanuri group of the Saharan branch of the Nilo-Saharan linguistic family; the other groups of the same branch are: the Teda-Daza, comprising Teda language for the people living in the Tibesti and its surroundings and Daza for those living in the sandy areas; and the Zaghawa-Berti group, these languages being spoken by the people of eastern Chad and Darfur in modern Sudan Republic. It is almost universally accepted today that Kanuri language developed from Ancient Kanembu following a linguistic drift generated by several combined historical factors such as migration from the eastern to the western shore of Lake Chad, the integration of other ethnic groups of Chadic speakers and the development of a centralized and expansionist socio-political system (Smith 1976). Data from comparative lexicons were collected by Barth and Nachtigal during their expeditions in the nineteenth century and, in what is considered by some German scholars and the editor of his works (Fisher and Fisher in Nachtigal 1980: 453), as the most difficult and interesting part of his accounts, Nachtigal had attempted to frame the historical connections between the different languages of the Central Sudan.

Until very recently, that is until there was proof of the linguistic relationship between Tubu and Kanuri, the Tubu, in view of their physical characteristics and many other of their customs and usages, were generally included among the Berbers. Why should Leo and some of the Arab writers, who were even less aware than we are today of the linguistic differences between the two, and in the Sahara knew only Arabs, Berbers and Negroes, not have done the same? (Nachtigal 1980: 461)

Nachtigal was struck by what he considered genuine similarities between Kanuri and Teda languages and devised a hypothesis to explain the causes of the observed linguistic features: 'the starting point of the language of Bornu also is to a large extent to be sought in Tu - Tibesti - the heartland of the Tubu' (Nachtigal 1980: 465). For our research purpose, there are two important points in these early historical linguistic enquiries of Nachtigal: the first is his conjecture about the existence of a broad North African language group which was later confirmed and termed Saharan Languages, and the second is his clear distinction between a Teda-Daza-Kanuri branch and a Baele-Zaghawa branch which had diverged at an unknown but very remote period.

It appears indubitable to me that the Teda dialect is the most ancient idiom of this group, that the foundation, derived from it, for Kanuri probably branched off a very long time ago, and Dazaga only later, and that these two have developed further without significant contact with each other. Although Baele (and with it the Zoghawa language) is more distant from Tubu and Kanuri than these are from each other, and although precisely the investigation of Baele and the comparison between it and other Sudan languages considerably widened the range of my thinking and led to the conjecture of a broad North African language group which may embrace a large part of the Sahara and Sudan. (Nachtigal 1980: 476-477)

More recent linguistic studies have improved the research methods and the classification of languages from the Central Sudan (Dalby 1980, Greenberg 1980, Thelwall 1982, Wolff 1987) and interesting discussions on the reliability of inferred genetic relationships between different languages are always going on among linguists. In his recent work, Nicolaï (1990) has shown that Songhay, which was and still is considered by some researchers as a Saharan language, had in fact resulted from the combination of a 'pidginized' form of Tuareg - a Berber language - shaped within the mould of Mande. This research thus suggests the possibility of the emergence of a new language from the hybridization of languages belonging to different linguistic families, a finding which runs counter one of the axioms of historical linguistics: 'there is no linguistic hybridization in the sense of mixed ancestry for particular languages' (Wolff 1987: 30).

As far as Saharan languages are concerned, we may hypothesize from the Tibesti-Ennedi, an early split between an southeastern branch - the proto-Zaghawa/Berti group - a northwestern branch - the proto-Teda/Daza group - and a south/southwestern branch - the proto Kanembu group -.This early drift was followed by another which initiated the development of present-days languages of the Central Sudan with the split between Zaghawa and Berti language in the proto-Zaghawa/Berti group in the southeast, Tedaga and Dazaga from the proto-Teda/Daza group in the centre, north and northwest, and Kanuri and Kanembu from the proto-Kanembu group, mostly distributed in the south and southwest. Kanuri language appears as the most extended in the southwestern direction, mostly in contact with speakers of western and central Chadic languages and

Fulani, an expansion which may have started with the early settlements of the Yobe flood-plain in c. 750-900. If the results achieved by Nicolaï (1990: 183-8) on the dual Tuareg and Mande origin of the Songhay languages are confirmed by further research, his approach, based on the evaluation of different states of languages which may, according to actual social, economic and political, or for short socio-linguistic circumstances, shift from a vernacular form - or localized dialect - to a vehicular one - or lingua franca - if adopted for the study of other languages from Central Sudan, may shed new light and, maybe, clarify some important aspects of the history of the formation of the Kanuri language in its long-lasting interaction with Chadic languages.

Part Six

Kanuri Domination and Literacy

Chapter 14

A Model for the Emergence of Kanuri Domination

The version of the Diwan looked at has been shown to be one among many; it is a highly complex web of social, ideological and political claims of one part of the Kanuri social formation. Our study has also shown that the document pertains to a local theory of cyclical history, initiated by a Golden Age (Sequence I), then followed by a Classic Period (Sequence II) and the collapse of the system in a First Intermediate Period (Sequence III) and, finally, the rise of civilization with the New Kingdom (Sequence IV) centred at Ghazzargamo. The system portrayed by the Diwan is basically that of the emergence of Kanuri domination and their 'Manifest Destiny'. In order to build another model for the emergence of the Bornu state many parameters have to taken into account: the structural changes of social systems, transformations of subsistence and socio-economic system within the context of changing environmental patterns and the system of domination which may have developed by early Kanuri settlers of the Yobe flood-plain (Eisenstadt et al. 1988).

As discussed previously, during Sequences I and II, the rise to paramount chiefship was based on a network of alliance between four ethnic groups or high-ranked lineages which were basically equal; sultans were only primus inter pares and their residences shifted according the vagaries of the network of allied groups. Some prestations due to the paramount chief and a small amount of tribute may have been extracted from the lower-ranked lineages of wife-givers. the succession of multiple cycles of alliance through marriage and the inclusion of an increasing numbers of lineages in the system resulted in the multiplication of potential heirs to paramount chiefship and younger collateral chiefly lines. In the relatively desert-like environment of Kanem, human settlements were widely dispersed into localized lineage territories and the socio-political system devised seems to have been an open one, with lowest-ranked lineages of wife-givers linked to highest-ranked wife-takers. Such 'open systems are closely correlated with political and economic expansion, where the population included in the circles expands and where there is consequently a multiplication of new lineage segments' (Friedman 1984: 169). Through lineage fissioning, kin are continually transformed into potential allies. But the main problem within this social strategy is the internal contradiction between the transitivity of indebtedness and the relative closure of the marriage circle implied in the asymmetrical relationship between wife-givers and wife-takers (Friedman 1984, Friedman and Rowlands 1977). As attested in Sequence II of the Diwan, princes Abd Allah Bakuru and Batku, sons of Sultan Bir (reign 14), received gifts of 100 camels each when they went to visit their mother Ghumsa F.sama, daughter of S.karam of the tribe of M.gh.r.ma, at Khayr.k.r.s.mu. Abd Allah Bakuru took the succeeded to his father as the fifteenth sultan and his brother Batku became the headman of the tribe of the M.gh.r.ma. The latter's daughter Dabali was married by Sultan Salmama (reign 16) who had initiated the development of a new lineage or descent group, and was succeeded by his son Dunama (reign 17) (Figure 20). With reign 20 of Sultan Ibrahim, the marriage circle seems to have been definitely closed, as suggested by the systematic lack of any reference to mothers' fathers and even mothers' names.

The functioning of this system transforms the egalitarian marriage circles into a political and economic hierarchy of wife-givers and wife-takers. The end-product is not, of course, a simple transitive ordering but, rather, a regrouping of lineages into more or less closed circles of allies capable of paying a similar bridge-price, i.e., a spiral ranking, where at each level there are a number of lineages of approximately equal status. (Friedman 1984: 171)

The three descent groups reconstructed in Sequence II (see Figure 7), the Banu Abd al Djalil, the Banu Salmama and the Banu Kaday, embracing two to five generations, can be considered as lineages of approximately equal status. However, from the middle of

Sequence II, under the reign of Dunama (17) who had commited the outrageous act of opening the <u>Muni</u>, serious difficulties started for the whole system and in Sequence III, warring fractions emerged leading to the exodus of some high-ranked lineages. It may be argued that these events referred to the collapse of the former system built upon a confederation of equal lineages, a collapse accelerated by the introduction and the radical implementation of Islam which may have raised strong opposition from other highest- and lowest-ranked lineages. The groups opposed to the ruling lineage were therefore collectively labelled Bulala, to ascribe them with another identity. The ruling lineage which had emigrated to the Yobe flood-plain in the second half of the fourteenth century, was not properly in an alien land, as earlier groups of Kanembu speakers were already settled there from 750 AD. Contacts between the eastern and western shores of Lake Chad was easy during the dry seasons; it is therefore suggested that the Kanembu diaspora from the Yobe area may have been well aware of the political situation in Kanem and that there were both supporters and opponents of the fleeing Sayfawa rulers. The desiccation of lake Chad in c. 1350-1450 accelerated the reorganization of settlement patterns and modified the distribution of population on the Kanem and Bornu shores of Lake Chad. Higher densities of population were confined to river valleys such as the Bahr el Ghazzal and the Yobe River, which were the focal areas for the development of two competing social systems, that of the Bulala in the east and that later termed Kanuri in the west.

The exodus to Bornu thus closed the cycles of confederation of allied lineages and initiated a new kind of socio-political system based on shifting balance of power between two competing collateral lines. It is worth emphasizing the fact that both warring collateral lines, or even lineages, the Banu Idris and the Banu Dawud, had left Kanem and settled in Bornu. The main condition for survival for the ruling and prestigeous lineages was probably the ability to attract followers, gain their support and then expand their influence in the different proto-Kanuri settlements. Through demographic increase, the practice of preferential marriage, the absorption of other ethnic groups, warfare, the expansion of chiefly ideology and Islam, a new cultural group with a new idiom derived from the Kanembu language emerged on the western shore of Lake Chad, established its capital city at Ghasrakmu - Birni Ghazzargamo - and created the famous kingdom of Bornu.

The processes implied in this development are as yet very poorly understood, partly because of the lack of relevant sources of information. To model this important stage of the emergence of Kanuri domination, we will have to rely on social anthropology (Friedman 1984, Friedman and Rowlands 1977, Gluckman, 1950, 1955, Leach 1964, Southall 1970). In his research on the Alur, a Luo-speaking society in Uganda, Southall (1970: 7) has sought to explain how 'a new tribe has emerged out of a complex mixture of diverse groups over a comparatively short period'. For the study presented here, the case of the Alur is almost paradigmatic, even if similar processes have been recorded by Gluckman (1950, 1955) among the Lozi in Zambia. 'The process of Alur domination consisted in the spread of the Alur concept of chiefship, by means of the natural increase and spatial dispersion of the persons through whom it could be expressed' (Southall 1970: 181). Three major aspects of this process of domination are singled out : (1) the sustained increase in the number of chieflets, backed by the geometric rise of chiefs' and chieflets' lineages; these individuals and groups enjoyed the prestige and the privileges attached to chiefship; (2) Alur commoner clans, as the earliest subjects of Alur chiefs, by their exaction of rights and submission to obligations, demonstrated the practice of chiefship; and (3) the sections of non-Alur tribes on the moving frontiers of Alur chiefdoms, which considered it worthwhile to be integrated within the context of subject clans as junior members, slowly acquired equal status and full membership of Alur society. The dissemination of the sons of chiefs throughout the territory and its different settlements was instrumental in the expansion and adoption of the Alur type of socio-political organization

Groups entering this system exchanged a lower for a higher order of political organization, and exchanged a system of value which left them without any refuge from vagaries of climate and resulting famine for one in which they put confidence in the ecological control of the dominant group to which they have freely given their allegiance. (Southall 1970: 246)

The political system of the Alur was termed a segmentary state in which territorial sovereignty is recognized but limited and essentially relative; authority being strong at the centre and restricted in the peripheries. Government and administration exist in embryonic forms and the legitimate use of force is claimed and successfully implemented to a limited extent. Segmentary states as presented above, are fragile structures of great flexibility; however, this does not mean that they are always transitory, as they may last for a very long time. If we now shift back to our case study, it appears that in Sequence III, there was fighting between Sultan Bir (reign 34), son of

Idris and Kayghama Muhammad, probably a local title-holder: Sultan Uthman K.l.n.ma (reign 35), son of Dawud, was dismissed by a coalition of Kayghama Nikali andYerima Kaday Ka^caku. Sultan Abd Allah (reign 37), son of Umar was moved from office by Kayghama Abd Allah D.gh.l.ma, and restored to power after the death of Sultan Ibrahim (reign 38), son of Uthman. And finally, Sultan Ghadji (reign 44) was slain by Kanema Muhammad. It may be inferred that some members of the local groups were allied to one lineage or the other and attempted to control access to chiefship. The toponyms for the places of death or burial of the Sayfawa chiefs suggest that they were moving from one place to another in search of a safer residence, which ultimately would be found at Ghazzargamo, the capital of the New Kingdom of Bornu, during the reign of Sultan Ali, son of Dunama (48), thus initiating the begining of the fourth sequence. It is therefore not surprising that with the arrival at Ghazzargamo, the internal war ended with the murder of Sultan Uthman, son of Kaday, the last rival from the Dawud lineage, slain by Sultan Ali himself. With the new system, there was only one ruling lineage which was be segmented in sub-lineages. The new era was characterized by the development of religion, learning, peace and prosperity, and even external wars ended with the defeat of the Bulala during the reign of Idris, son of Ali (54). The unitary state, based on the organizing principles of Islam, launched an endless series of wars against neighbouring ethnic groups, for conquest, extraction of tribute and booty. The political organization of the kingdom was constituted of different components: the core of the kingdom, with its capital at the centre, was the centralized government and administration. The exclusive use of force for the state was implemented with the development of an army, with cavalry as elite troops, archers and later musketeers. On the 'inner' periphery were the territories of the allied and conquered ethnic groups. They were ruled directly by appointees of the king under the supervision of some highest-ranked officials, members of the ruling council of the kingdom, such as the Kayghama for southern territories and the Yerima for western territories. On the outer periphery, there were the territories of dependants subject to a regular payment of tribute. Beyond these limits, which were always fluctuating due to shifts in alliance and the vagaries of the rise and fall of local polities, were the lands subjected to endemic raiding for booty. The wealth of kingdom was partly based on the endless cycles of predatory accumulation (Reyna 1990) and the balance of power between competing kingdoms such as the Barma state, Songhay, the Hawsa polities and later those of the Wadday. Following the expansion of the Bornu kingdom, the Kanuri language became a lingua franca in the central part of Central Sudan. The development of religion and learning expanded litteracy among the members of the Kanuri elite, and different historical versions of the fate and deeds of the Sayfawa were transmitted in oral form from one generation to the next, and some of them, such as the version studied here, were put into written form later, in the first half of the nineteenth century. The proposition presented by Leach forty years ago, about the Kachin traditions is equally true for the Kanuri.

I think social anthropologists only tend to think of myth systems as internally consistent because they retain something of the ethnologist's notion that myth is a kind of history. Because of this prejudice they come to be selective in their analysis of myth and tend to discriminate between 'correct' and 'incorect' versions of the same tale... In the case of Kachin mythology there can be no possibility of eliminating the contradictions and inconsistencies. They are fundamental. Where there are rival versions of the same story, no one version is 'more correct' than any other. On the contrary, I hold that the contradictions are more significant than the uniformities. (Leach 1964: 265).

It would be highly interesting to make an in-depth comparative study of the different kings' lists available today for the Bornu ruling dynasty. As shown in the present research, the Diwan is but a small part of the different social strategies used to lay the foundation for competing claims for legitimacy; it is, in effect a fragment of the Kanuri theory of history which needs a complex interpretation.

Epilogue

The Diwan : An Epic of the Sayfawa

If as suggested by the discussions conducted in this work and the understanding gained from other sources (Goody and Goody 1992, Njoya 1989, Schmidt 1978, 1983a, Wilks et al. 1986, Yacine 1987), the Diwan is better considered as part of the social memory of the Kanuri people (Connerton 1989). It is basically syncretic in nature and combines aspects of the <u>Hadith</u>, lessons from the Koran, with Kanuri systems of values. The different versions collected and studied during the last one hundred and fifty years probably result from a diversity of social circumstances within a dynamic social and political system, and were geared to conflicting or complementary claims for legitimacy, knowledge of the 'genuine past' and performativeness. The kings lists were performed as piece of epic poetry - an eternal poeticized history - and centred on the fate and deeds of the Sayfawa dynasty, with their 'inconsistencies', contradictions and diversity of versions. It is therefore easy to understand why a simple and single-minded attempt to extract 'genuine' historical information is doomed to failure. The Diwan was probably presented in a particular Kanuri speech, accessible to those who were initiated or able to listen and understand the 'pure' words of deep-time traditions, and constructed within a rhythmic frame. As suggested by Okpewho (1979: 66), the heroic song appears to be an ever-living event, the bard or the performer being continually obliged to use contemporary material and so frequently altering the old form of the song. Consequently:

Although he is working with old traditional material, he is so eager to make an impression on the contemporary audience that he is led to rework some of that material. Often he is unaware of this violation of his ancient truth; what counts for him is more the continued relevance and appeal of his song. (Okpewho 1979: 66)

The fundamental oral nature of epics clearly highlighted by some famous West and Central African examples such as the chronicle of Wagadou for the Ghana kingdom (Dieterlen and Sylla 1992), the Epic of Sunjata for early Mali kingdom (Cissé and Kamissoko 1988), and many others (Ngijol 1980, Okpewho 1979, Vansina 1990) has posed serious difficulties to students of African history.

That very characteristic presented problems for transcription and interpretation, leaving more play for the intervention of the scribe's imagination, making it more difficult to construct a fixed text out of a fixed utterance. The gap between oral utterance and written text, between text and translation, may be wide, much wider than with the other material. (Goody and Goody 1992: 269)

In this regard, it may be considered that the scribes who wrote downtwo copies of the Diwan for a foreigner - H. Barth - do not seem to have cared about the poetry of the narrative. The epic was simply framed as an ordinary account, thus transmuting poetry into 'tasteless' mundane prose. In the prologue of this study, the Diwan is frame as closely as possible in the form of the vanished poetry following syntax rules outlined in our discussion, with each key formula situated at the beginning of an approximative verse. With all its imperfections, of which we are aware, it is hoped that this reconstitution restores a part of the lost poetic flavour. As this work is based on a French translation of Kanuri epic originally written in Arabic, the result presented is to be considered simply as an heuristic test case.

131

BIBLIOGRAPHY

Adams, W.Y. (1982) The coming of Nubian speakers to the Nile valley, in The Archaeological and Linguistic Reconstruction of African History, edited by Ch. Ehret and M. Posnansky, Berkeley, University of California Press, pp. 11-38.

Alexandre, P. (1982) African political systems revisited, Cahiers d'études Africaines XXII, 87-8 (3-4): 299-330.

Baroin, C. (1985) Anarchie et cohésion sociale chez les Toubou: les Daza Késerda (Niger), Paris/Cambridge, Editions de la Maison des Sciences de l'Homme/ Cambridge University Press.

Barth, F. (ed.) (1969) Ethnic Groups and Boundaries: The Social Organization of Culture Difference, Oslo, Universiteitsforlaget Bergen.

(1973) Descent and marriage reconsidered, in The Character of Kinship, edited by J. Goody, Cambridge, Cambridge University Press, pp. 3-20.

Barth, H. (1965) Travels and Discoveries in North and Central Africa, Vol. II. London, Frank Cass.

Bateson, G. and M.C. Bateson (1988) Angels Fear: Toward an Epistemology of the Sacred, New York, Bantam Books.

Bathily, A. (1977) Intervention, in Actes du Colloque Histoire et Tradition Orale, Fondation SCOA pour la recherche scientifique en Afrique noire, Paris, pp. 114-15.

Bernus, S. and P. Cressier (eds) (1991) La Région d'In Gall - Tegidda n Tesemt (Niger) IV: Azelik-Takadda et l'implantation sédentaire médiévale, Niamey, Etudes Nigériennes No 51.

Bisson, M.S. (1982) Trade and tribute: archaeological evidence for the origin of state in South Central Africa, Cahiers d'études Africaines XXII, 87-8 (3-4): 343-61.

Bivar, A.D.H. and P.L. Shinnie (1962) 'Old Kanuri capitals' Journal of African History 3(1): 1-10.

Blanton, R. E. (1976) Anthropological studies of cities, Annual Review of Anthropology 5: 249-64.

Blanton, R.E., J. Appel, L. Finsten, S. Kowalewski, G. Feinman and E. Fisch (1979) Regional evolution in the valley of Oaxaca, Mexico, Journal of Field Archaeology 6: 367-90.

Blanton, R.E., S. A. Kowalewski, G. Feinman and J. Appel (1981) Ancient Mesoamrica: A comparison of changes in three regions, Cambridge/New York, Cambridge University Press.

Blench, R.E. (1991) The Dessication of lake Chad-1990, Paper presented at the Mega-Chad Network Conference, L'Homme et le Milieu Végétal, 18-20 Sept. 1991, Sèvres, France.

Blount, B. G. (1975) Agreeing to agree on genealogy: a Luo sociology of knowledge, in Sociocultural Dimensions of Language Use, edited by M. Sanchez and B.G. Blount, New York, Academic Press, pp. 117-35.

Boahen, A. (1986) Etre historien aujourd'hui: la perspective africaine, in Etre historien aujourd'hui: l'histoire et les historiens de l'Afrique contemporaine, Actes du Colloque de Nice, Paris, UNESCO, pp. 255-67.

Bohannan, P. and L. Bohannan (1968) Tiv Economy, London, Longmans.

Bonte, P. and E. Conte (1991) La Tribu arabe: Approches anthropologiques et orientalistes, in,Al-Ansab: la Quête des Origines: Anthropologie Historique de la Société Tribale Arabe, P. Bonte, E.Conte, C. Hamès and Abdel Wedoud Ould Cheikh, Paris, Editions de la Maison des Sciences de l'Homme, pp. 13-54.

Bonte, P., E. Conte, C. Hamès and Abdel Wedoud ould Cheikh (1991) Al-Ansab: la Quête des Origines: Anthropologie Historique de la Société Tribale Arabe, Paris, Editions de la Maison des Sciences de l'Homme.

Borgström, B. E. (1977) On rank and hierarchy: status in India and elsewhere, Archives Européennes de Sociologie, 18: 325-34.

Bovill, E. W. (1978)The Golden Trade of the Moors, London, Oxford University Press.

Brenner, L. (1973) The Shehus of Kukawa: A History of the Al-Kanemi Dynasty of Bornu, Oxford, Oxford University Press.

Briant, P. (1982) Etat et Pasteurs au Moyen Orient Ancien , London/Paris, Cambridge University Press, Maison des Sciences de l'Homme.

Butzer, K.W. (1981) Rise and Fall of Axum, Ethiopia: A geo-archaeological interpretation, American Antiquity 46: 471-95.

Cahiers d'études Africaines (1992) Special Issue 'African Political Systems Revisited' Cahiers d'études Africaines XXII, 87-8.

Cancian, F. (1976) Social stratification, Annual Review of Anthropology 5: 227-48.

Carneiro, R.L. (1981) The chiefdom: precursor of the state, in G.D. Jones and R.R. Kautz (eds.), in Transition to Statehood in the New World, Cambridge/New York, Cambridge University Press, pp. 37-79.

Cissé, Y.T. and W. Kamissoko (1988) La Grande Geste du Mali, Paris, Karthala-Arsan.

Chang, K. C. (1983) Art, Myth, and Ritual: The Path to Political Authority in Ancient China, Cambridge MA. Harvard University Press.

Chapelle, J. (1982) Nomades noirs du Sahara: les Toubous, Paris, L'Harmattan.

Chapman, R. (1990) Emerging Complexity, Cambridge, Cambridge University Press.

Chrétien, J.-P. (1989) Variantes et points de fixation dans le récits historiques du Burundi, in Sources orales de l'histoire de l'Afrique, edited by Cl. H. Perrot, G. Gonnin and F. Nahimana, Paris, CNRS, pp. 193-208.

Claessen, H. J. M. (1984) The internal dynamics of early states, Current Anthropology 25: 365-79.

Claessen, H.J.M and P. van de Velde (eds.) (1987) Early States Dynamics , Leiden, E.J. Brill.

Cohen, A. (1969) Political anthropology: the analysis of the symbolism of power relations, Man 2: 215-235.

_ (1974a) Introduction: the lesson of ethnicity, in Urban Ethnicity, edited by A. Cohen, London, Tavistock, pp. ix-xxiv.

_ (1974b) Two-Dimensional Man, London Routledge and Kegan Paul.

Cohen, R. (1966) The Bornu king lists, Boston University Papers in African History 2: 39-84.

Connah, G. (1969a) Archaeological Worki in Bornu 1964-1966 with particular Reference to the Excavations at Daima Mound, in Actes du Premier International d'Archéologie Africaine, edited by J.P. Lebeuf, Fort-Lamy, INTSH, pp. 112-124.

_ (1969b) Settlement Mounds of the Firki - The Reconstruction of a Lost Society, Ibadan 26: 48-62.

_ (1971) Recent Contributions to Bornu Chronology, West African Journal of Archaeology 1: 55-60.

_ (1981) Three Thousand Years in Africa: Man and his Environment in the Lake Chad Region of Nigeria, Cambridge, Cambridge University Press.

_ (1984) An Archaeological Exploration in Southern Borno, The African Archaeological Review 2: 153-71.

_ (1985) Agricultural Intensification and Sedentism in the Firki of N.E. Nigeria, in Prehistoric Intensive Agriculture in the Tropics: Vol. II, edited by I.S. Farrington, Oxford, British Archaeological Reports, pp. 765-786.

Connah, G. and S.J. Freeth (1989) A Commodity Problem in Prehistoric Borno, Sahara 2: 7-20.

Connerton, P. (1989) How Societies Remember, Cambridge, Cambridge University Press.

Conrad, G.W. and A.A. Demarest (1984) Religion and Empire: The Dynamics of Aztec and Inca Expansion, Cambridge/New York, Cambridge University press.

Conte, E. (1979) Politics and Marriage in South Kanem (Chad): A Statistical Presentation of Endogamy from 1895 to 1975, Cahiers ORSTOM série Sciences Humaines 16(4): 275-97.

Coppens, Y. (1969) Les cultures protohistoriques et historiques du Djourab, in Actes du Premier International d'Archéologie Africaine, edited by J.P. Lebeuf, Fort-Lamy, INTSH, pp. 129-46.

Le Coran (1970) Translated by Kasimirski, Paris, Garnier-Flammarion.

Cordell, D. D. (1985) The Awlad Sulayman of Libya and Chad: Power and Adaptation in the Sahara and the Sahel, in Les Défricheurs de l'Islam en Afrique Occidentale, edited by B. Jewsiewicki and J.-L. Triaud, Quebec, pp. 319-43.

Crump, T. (1992) The Anthropology of Numbers, Cambridge, Cambridge University Press.

Cuoq, J. (1984) Histoire de l'Islamisation de l'Afrique de l'Ouest des origines à la fin du XVIe siècle, Paris, Paul Geuthner.

Dalby, D. (1980) Carte linguistique de l'Afrique, in Histoire Générale de l'Afrique I: Méthodologie et Préhistoire Africaine, edited by J. Ki-Zerbo, Paris, UNESCO, pp. 339-46.

D'Arbaumont, J. (1989a) Le Tibesti et le Domaine Teda - Daza, Paris, Centre d'études sur l'histoire du Sahara.

_ (1989b) Organisation Politique au Tibesti: Une Convention entre Arna et Tomagra, Paris, Centre d'études sur l'histoire du Sahara.

De Morais-Farias, P. (1990) The oldest extant writing of West Africa: medieval epigraphs from Essuk, Saney, and Egef-n-Tawaqqast (Mali), Journal des Africanistes 60(2): 65-113.

Denham, Dixon, Captain H. Clapperton and Dr Oudney (1826) <u>Narrative of Travels and Discoveries in Northern and Central Africa in the Years 1822,1823 and 1824,</u> London , J. Murray.

Dieterlen, G. and D. Sylla (1992) <u>L'empire de Ghana: Le Wagadou et les traditions de Yéréré</u>, Paris, Karthala-Arsan.

Doolittle, W.E. (1984) Settlements and the development of 'statelets' in Sonora, Mexico, <u>Journal of Field</u> Archaeology 11: 13-24.

Dragadze, T. (1980) The place of 'Ethnos' theory in Soviet Anthropology, in <u>Soviet and Western Anthropology,</u> edited by E. Gellner, London, Duckworth, p. 161-70.

Dumont, L. (1966) <u>Homo Hierarchicus: le système des castes et ses implications,</u> Paris, Gallimard.

_ (1977) <u>Homo Aequalis: génèse et épanouissement de l'idéologie économique,</u> Paris, Gallimard.

_ (1983) <u>Essais sur l'individualisme: une perspective anthropologique sur l'idéologie moderne ,</u> Paris, Editions du Seuil.

Duncan, J. (1981) Introduction, in <u>Housing and Identity: Cross-Cultural Perspectives,</u> edited by J.S. Duncan, London, Croom Helm, p. 1-5.

Eisenstadt, S.N., M. Abitbol and N. Chazan (1983) Les origines de l'état: une nouvelle approche, <u>Annales: Economie Sociétés Civilisations</u> 6: 1232-55.

Eisenstadt, S.N., M Abitbol and N. Chazan (eds) 1988) <u>The Early State in African Perspective: Culture, Power and Division of Labour,</u> Leiden, E.J. Brill.

Etienne, B. (1987) <u>L'Islamisme Radical,</u> Paris, Hachette.

Fisher, H.J. (1975) The Central Sahara and Sudan, in <u>The Cambridge History of Africa 4: from c.1600 to c. 1790,</u> edited by R. Gray, Cambridge, Cambridge University Press, pp. 58-141.

_ (1977) The Eastern Maghrib and the Central Sudan, in <u>The Cambridge History of Africa 3: from c. 1050 to c. 1600,</u> edited by R. Oliver, Cambridge, Cambridge University Press,pp.232-331.

_ (1987) Review article: Sudanese and Saharan Studies, <u>Journal of African History</u> 28: 281-293.

Fortes, M. (1969) <u>Kinship and the Social Order,</u> London, Routledge and Kegan Paul.

Fortes, M. and E.E. Evans-Pritchard (eds) (1940), <u>African Political Systems,</u> Oxford, Oxford University Press. (Reprinted 1967.)

Freedman, D.N. (n.d.) Kingly chronologies: then and later, <u>Eretz Israel</u> .

Friedman, J. (1984) Tribes, States, and Transformations, in Marxist Analyses and Social Anthropology, edited by Maurice Bloch, London, Tavistock, pp. 161-202.

Friedman, J. and M.J. Rowlands (1977) Notes towards an epigenetic model of the evolution of 'civilisation', The Evolution of Social Systems, edited by J. Friedman and M.J. Rowlands, London, Duckworth, pp. 201-76.

Gaussen J. and M. Gaussen (1989) Le Tilemsi Préhistorique et ses abords: Sahara et Sahel Malien, Paris, Editions du CNRS.

Gellner, E. (1977) Class before state: the Soviet treatment of African feudalism, Archives Européennes de Sociologie 18: 299-322.

Gluckman, M. (1950) Kinship and marriage among the Lozi of Northern Rhadesia and the Zulu of Natal, in African Systems of Kinship and Marriage, edited by A.R. Radcliffe-Brown & Daryll Forde, Oxford, Oxford University Press, pp.166-206.

_ (1955) Custom and Conflict in Africa, Oxford, Blackwell.

Godelier, M. (1977) Horizons et Trajets Marxistes en Anthropologie I, Paris, F. Maspéro.

_ (1980) The concept of 'Asiatic Mode of Production' and Marxist models of social evolution, in Relations of Production, edited by D. Seddon, London, F. Cass, pp. 209-57.

Goody, J. (ed.) (1973) The Character of Kinship, Cambridge, Cambridge University Press.

_ (1980) Technology, Tradition and the State in Africa, Cambridge/New York, Cambridge University Press.

Goody, E. and J. Goody (1992) Creating a Text: alternative interpretations of Gonja drum history, Africa 11(2): 266-270.

Greenberg, J. H. (1980) Classification des langues d'Afrique, in Histoire Générale de l'Afrique I: Méthodologie et Préhistoire Africaine, edited by J. Ki-Zerbo, Paris, UNESCO, pp.321-338.

Grébénart, D. (1985) La Région d'In Gall-Tegidda n Tesemt (Niger) II: Le Néolithique Final et les débuts de la Métallurgie, Niamey, Etudes Nigériennes, No 49.

Grove, A.T. (1978) Geographical introduction to the Sahel, Geographical Journal 144: 401-15.

_ (1985) Water characteristics of the Chari system and Lake Chad, in The Niger and its Neighbours, edited by A.T.Grove, Rotterdam, A.A. Balkema, pp. 61-76.

Haas, J. (1981) Class conflict and the state in the New World, in G.D. Jones and R.R. Kautz (eds.), The Transition to Statehood in the New World, Cambridge/New York, Cambridge University Press, pp. 80-102.

_ (1982) The Evolution of Prehistoric State , New York, Columbia University Press.

Hallam, W.K.R. (1966) The Bayajida legend in Hausa legend, Journal of African History 7(1): 47-60.

Henige, D.P. (1971) Oral tradition and chronology, Journal of African History XII (3): 371-389.

_ (1982) Oral Historiography, London, Longman.

Hjort, A. (1981) Ethnic transformations, dependency and change: the Iligira Samburu of northern Kenya, in Change and Development in Nomadic and Pastoral Societies, edited by J.C. Galaty and P.C. Salzman, Leiden, E.J. Brill, pp. 50-67.

Holl, A. (1985) Background to the Ghana Empire: Archaeological investigations on the transition to statehood in the Dhar Tichitt region (Mauritania), Journal of Anthropological Archaeology 4: 73-115.

_ (1987) Mound Formation Processes and Societal Transformations: A case Study from the Perichadian Plain, Journal of Anthropological Archaeology 6: 122-158.

_ (1988a) Transition du néolithique à l'Age du Fer dans la plaine péritchadienne: le cas de Mdaga, in Le Milieu et les Hommes: Recherches Comparatives et Historiques dans le Bassin du lac Tchad, edited by D. Barreteaux and H. Tourneux, Paris, Editions de l'ORSTOM, pp. 81-109.

_ (1988b) Houlouf I: Archéologie des Sociétés Protohistoriques du Nord-Cameroun, Oxford, British Archaeological Reports, Cambridge Monographs in African Archaeology.

_ (1989) Individus et Statuts: Variabilité mortuaire dans la plaine tchadienne préhistorique, Singularités: Les voies d'émergence individuelles, Paris, Plon, pp. 351-367.

_ (1990) Variabilité mortuaire et transformations culturelles dans la plaine tchadienne, Relations Interethniques et Culture Matérielle dans le Bassin du lac Tchad, edited by D. Barreteau and H. Tourneux, Paris, Editions de l'ORSTOM, pp. 13-33.

_ (1992) Systématique archéologique et processus culturels: essai d'archéologie régionale dans le secteur de Houlouf (Nord-Cameroun), L'Archéologie au Cameroun, edited by J.M. Essomba, Paris, Karthala, pp. 53-78.

_ (1993a) Ethnic Interaction and Settlement Patterning in Northern Cameroon, in Spatial Boundaries and Social Dynamics, edited by A.Holl and T.E. Levy, Ann Arbor, International Monographs in Prehistory, pp. 39-61.

_ (1993b) Late Neolithic cultural landscape in Southeastern Mauritania: An essay in spatiometrics, in Spatial Boundaries and Social Dynamics, edited by A.Holl and T.E. Levy, Ann Arbor, International Monographs in Prehistory, pp. 95-133.

_ (1994) The Cemetery of Houlouf: Fragments of a past Social System, The African Archaeological Review. 12: 133-70.

Hopkins, A.G. (1980) An Economic History of West Africa , London, Longman.

Itéanu, A. (1983) La ronde des échanges: de la circulation aux valeurs chez les Orokaïva, Cambridge/Paris, Cambridge University Press/Maison des Sciences de l'Homme.

Johnson, G.A. (1976) Early state organization in Southwest Iran: preliminary field report, in Proceedings of the IVth Annual Symposium on Archaeological Research in Iran , edited by F. Bagherzadeh, Tehran, pp. 190-223.

_ (1982) Organisationall structure and scalar stress, in Theory and Explanation in Archaeology, edited by C. Renfrew, M. J. Rowlands and B.A. Seegraves, London/New York, Academic Press, pp. 389-421.

_ (1987) The changing organization of Uruk administration on the Susiana plain, in The Archaeology of Western Iran, edited by F. Hole, Washington D.C., Smithsonian Institution Press, pp. 107-39.

Jones G.D. and R.R. Kautz (1981) Issues in the study of New World state formation, in The Transition to Statehood in the New World, edited by G.D. Jones and R.R. Kautz, Cambridge/New York, Cambridge University Press, pp. 3-34.

Keatinge, R.W. (1981) The nature and role of religious diffusion in the early stages of state formation: an example from Peruvian prehistory, in The Transition to Statehood in the New World, edited by G.D. Jones and R.R. Kautz, Cambridge/New York, Cambridge University Press, pp. 172-87.

Knutsson, K.E. (1969) Dichotomization and integration: aspects of interethnic relations in Southern Ethiopia, Ethnic Groups and Boundaries:The Social Organization of Culture Diffrence, edited by F. Barth, Oslo, Universiteitsforlaget Bergen, pp. 86-100.

Kowalewski, S.A., R.E. Blanton, G. Feinman and L. Finsten (1983) Boundaries, Scale, and internal organization, Journal of Anthropological Archaeology 2: 32-56.

Kropacek, L. (1985) La Nubie: de la fin du XIIe siècle à la conquête par les Funj au début du XVIe siècle, in Histoire Générale de l'Afrique, Vol. IV, edited by D.T. Niane, Paris, UNESCO/Nouvelles Editions Africaines, pp. 433-60.

Landeroin, M. A. (1911) Notice historique, Documents Scientifiques de la Mission Tilho 1906-1909, Paris, Imprimerie Nationale.

Lange, D. (1977) Chronologie et Histoire d'un Royaume Africain, Wiesbaden, Franz Steiner Verlag.

_ (1982) L'éviction des Sayfawa du Kanem et l'origine des Bulala, Journal of African History 23(3): 315-331.

_ (1985) Royaumes et peuples du Tchad, in Histoire Générale de l'Afrique IV: L'Afrique du XIIe au XVIe siècle, edited by D.T. Niane, Paris, UNESCO; pp. 265-292.

_ (1987) A Sudanic Chronicle: The Borno Expeditions of Idris Alauma (1564-1576), Wiesbaden, Fr. Steiner Verlag.

_ (1989) Préliminaires pour une histoire des Sao, Journal of African History 30(2): 189-210.

_ (1990) La Région du Tchad en tant que carrefour, in Histoire Générale de l'Afrique III: L'Afrique du VIIe au XIe siècle, edited by M. el Fasi and I. Hrbek, Paris, UNESCO, pp. 465-488.

Leach, E. R. (1964) Political Systems of Highland Burma: A Study of Kachin Social Structure, London, The Athlone Press.

_ (1973) Complementary filiation and bilateral kinship, *The Character of Kinship*, edited by J. Goody, Cambridge, Cambridge University Press, pp. 53-58.

Lebeuf, A.M.D. (1969) Les Principautés Kotoko: Essai sur le caractère sacré de l'autorité, Paris, CNRS.

- (1992) Le site de Sou: étude d'une aire d'activité domestique, L'Archéologie au Cameroun, edited by J-M Essomba, Paris, Karthala, pp. 79-89.

Lebeuf, J.-P. (1976) Etudes Kotoko, Paris / La Haye, Mouton.

_ (1992) Populations anciennes du Sud du lac Tchad, in L'Archéologie au Cameroun, edited by J-M Essomba, Paris, Karthala, pp. 91-99.

Lebeuf, J-P., A.M.D. Lebeuf, Fr. Treinen-Claustre and J. Courtin (1980) Le Gisement Sao de Mdaga: Fouilles 1960-1968, Paris, Société d'Ethnographie.

Levtzion, N. and J.F.P. Hopkins (eds.) (1981) Corpus of Early Arabic Sources for West African History, Cambridge, Cambridge University Press.

Levy, T.E. and A. Holl (1988) Les sociétés chalcolithiques de la Palestine et l'émergence des chefferies, Archives Européennes de Sociologie XXIX: 283-316.

Lewis, B. (1988) Le Langage Politique de l'Islam, Paris, Gallimard.

Lewis, I.M. (1980) Introduction: Islam in Tropical Africa. in Islam in Tropical Africa, edited by I.M.Lewis, London, Hutchinson, pp: 1-98.

Lovejoy, P. E. (1986) Salt of the Desert Sun: A History of Salt Production and Trade in the Central Sudan, Cambridge, Cambridge University Press.

Lowe-McConnell, R.H. (1985) The biology of the river systems with particular reference to the fishes, The Niger and its Neighbours, edited by A.T. Grove, Rotterdam, A.A. Balkema, pp. 134-42.

Maley, J. (1973) Les variations climatiques dans le bassin du Tchad durant le dernier millénaire: Nouvelles données palynologiques et paléoclimatiques, Le Quaternaire: Géodynamique, Stratigraphie et Environnement, Paris, Comité Français de l'INQUA, pp. 175-181.

_ (1981) Etudes Palynologiques dans le Bassin du Tchad et Paléoclimatologie de l'Afrique nord-tropicale de 30 000 ans à l'époque actuelle, Paris, Editions de l'ORSTOM.

Maley, J. and C. Seignobos (1989) Chronologie calendaire des principales fluctuations du lac Tchad au cours du dernier millénaire: le rôle des données historiques et de la tradition orale, paper presented at the Mega-Chad Network Seminar Datations et Chronologie dans le Bassin du Tchad, 10-11 Sept. 1989, Bondy, France.

Mauny, R. (1961)Tableau géographique de l'Ouest Africain au Moyen Age d'après les sources écrites, la tradition et l'archéologie, Dakar, Mémoires de l'IFAN No 61.

Mauss, M. (1990) The Gift, New York/London, W.W. Norton. (First published 1950.)

Meillassoux, Cl. (1980) The Economy' in agricultural self-sustaining societies: A preliminary analysis, in Relations of Production, edited by D. Seddon London, F. Cass, pp. 127-57.

Nachtigal, G. (1980) Sahara and Sudan Vol. II, translated and edited by A.G.B Fisher and H.J. Fisher, London, C. Hurst and Co.

Ngijol Ngijol, P. (1980) Les Fils de Hitong : I and II, Yaoundé, Centre d'édition et de production pour l'enseignement et la recherche.

Nicolaï, R. (1990) Parentés Linguistiques (à propos du Songhay), Paris, CNRS.

Nicholson, Sharon E. (1980) Saharan climates in historic times, inThe Sahara and the Nile, edited by M.A.J. Williams and H. Faure, Rotterdam, A.A. Balkema, pp.173-200.

Njoya, A. N. (1989) Chants dynastiques et chants populaires Bamum: sources d'informations historiques, Sources orales de l'histoire de l'Afrique, edited by Cl. H. Perrot, G. Gonnin and F. Nahimana, Paris, CNRS, pp. 65-77.

O'Fahey, R.S. (1993) Immunity and rivilege: Mahram and Zawiya in Sudanic Africa, paper presented at the Seminar 'State, Land and Society in Sudanic Africa,'' University of Illinois, Urbana-Champaign, April 23-5 1993

Okpewho, I. (1979)The Epic in Africa: Toward a Poetics of the Oral Performance, New York, Columbia University Press.

Oz, Amos (1993) In the Land of Israel, New York/London, Harcourt Brace and Co.

Palmer, H.R. (1928) Sudanese Memoirs, Lagos.

Perrot, Cl. H. (1989) Sources Orales et Histoire: un débat permanent, Sources orales de l'histoire de l'Afrique, edited by Cl. H. Perrot, G. Gonnin and F. Nahimana, Paris, CNRS, pp. 11-17.

Perrot Cl.H., G.Gonnin and F. Nahimana (eds.) (1989) Sources orales de l'histoire de l'Afrique, Paris, CNRS.

Phillipson, D.W. (1979) Migration, ethnic differentiation and state formation in the Iron Age of Bantu Africa, in Space, Hierarchy and Society, edited by B.C. Burnham and J. Kingsbury, Oxford, British Archaeological Reports, pp. 205-214.

Quilter, J. and T. Stocker (1983) Subsistence economies and the origins of Andean complex societies, American Anthropologist 85: 545-562.

Radcliffe-Brown, A.R. (1950) Introduction, African Systems of Kinship and Marriage, edited by A.R. Radcliffe-Brown and Daryll-Forde, Oxford, Oxford University Press, pp. 1-85.

Rapp, J. (1984) Quelques Aspects des civilisations néolithiques et post-néolithiques à l'extrême Nord-Cameroon: étude des décors céramiques et essai de chronologie, Unpubl. Doctorate thesis, University of Bordeaux I.

Renfrew, A.C. and J.F. Cherry (eds.) (1986) Peer-polity Interaction and Socio-political Change, Cambridge, Cambridge University Press.

Reyna, S. P. (1990) Wars without Ends: The Political Economy of a Precolonial African State, Hanover, University Press of New England.

Rodinson, M. (1961) Mahomet, Paris, Seuil.

Sahlins, M. D. (1968) Tribesmen, New Jersey, Prentice Hall.

_ (1976) Age de Pierre, âge d'abondance: l'économie des sociétés primitives, Paris, Gallimard.

_ (1985) Islands of History, Chicago, the University of Chicago Press.

Servant, M and S. Servant-Vildary (1973) Le Plio-Quaternaire du bassin du lac Tchad, Le Quaternaire: Geodynamique, Stratigraphie et Environnement, Paris, Comité Français de l'INQUA, pp. 167-175.

_ (1980) L'environnement quaternaire du bassin du lac Tchad, The Sahara and the Nile, edited by M.A.J. Williams and H. Faure, Rotterdam, A.A. Balkema, pp.133-62.

Schmidt, P.R. (1978) Historical archaeology: A Structural Approach on an African Culture, Westport, Greenwood Press.

_ (1983a) Cultural Meaning and History in African Myth, International Journal of Oral History 4(3): 167-183.

_ (1983b) An Alternative to a strictly Materialistic Perpective: A Review of Historical Archaeology, Ethnoarchaeology, and Symbolic Approaches in African Archaeology, American Antiquity 48(1): 62-79.

Smith, A. (1976) The early states of the Central Sudan, History of West Africa Vol. I, edited by J.F.A. Ajayi and M. Crowder, London, Longman, pp.152-93.

Southall, A. W. (1970) Alur Society: A Study in Processes and Types of Domination, Nairobi, Oxford University Press.

Steward, J.H. (1955) Theory of culture change: the methodology of multilinear evolution, Urbana, Chicago, London, University of Illinois Press.

Thelwall, R. (1982) Linguistic aspects of greater Nubian History, in The Archaeological and Linguistic Reconstruction of African History, edited by Ch. Ehret and M. Posnansky, Berkeley, University of California Press, pp. 39-52.

Thornton, J.K. (1982) The Kingdom of Kongo, ca. 1390-1678: the development of an African social formation, Cahiers d'Etudes Africaines XXII, 87-8 (3-4): 325-42.

Treinen-Claustre, Fr. (1978) Nouveaux éléments de datation absolue pour l'Age du fer de la région de Koro-Toro (Nord du Tchad), L'Anthropologie 82(1): 103-109.

_ (1982) Sahara et Sahel a l'Age du Fer: Borkou, Tchad, Paris, Société des Africanistes.

Trimingham, J.S. (1980) The Influence of Islam upon Africa (2nd edition), London, Longman.

Tyler, S. R. (1978) The Said and the Unsaid: Mind, Meaning and Culture; New York, Academic Press.

Urvoy, Y. (1949) Histoire de l'Empire du Bornou, Paris, Larose.

Vansina, J. (1985) Oral Tradition as History, London, James Currey.

_ (1990) Paths in the Rainforests: Toward a History of Political Tradition in Equatorial Africa , Madison, The University of Wisconsin Press.

Vernant, J.-P. (1974) Mythe et Société en Grèce Ancienne, Paris, La Découverte.

Walsh, C.E. (1983) Saving in primitive economies, American Anthropologist 85: 643-649.

Warnier, J.P. (1983) Sociologie du Bamenda Pré-colonial (Cameroun), Doctorate d'Etat thesis, University of Paris X Nanterre.

Wickins, P. (1981) An economic history of Africa from the earliest time to partition, Capetown, Oxford University Press.

Wilks, I., N.Levtzion and B.M. Haight (1986) Chronicles from Gonja: A Tradition of West African Muslim Historiography, Cambridge, Cambridge University Press.

Wittfogel, K. (1957) Le Despotisme oriental , Paris, Editions de Minuit. (New edition 1977.)

Wolff, E. (1987) Introductory Remarks on the Linguistic Situation in the Lake Chad Basin and the Study of Language Contact, in Langues et Cultures dans le Bassin du Lac Tchad, edited by D. Barreteau, Paris; Editions de l'ORSTOM, pp. 23-41.

Wright, H.T. (1977) Recent research on the origin of state, Annual Review of Anthropology 6: 379-397.

_ (1986) The evolution of civilisation, in American Archaeology: Past and Future, edited by D.J. Meltzer, D.D. Fowler and J.A. Sabloff, Washington /London, Smithsonian Institution Press, pp. 323-65.

Wright, H.T. and G.A. Johnson (1975) Population, exchange and early state formation in Southwestern Iran, American Anthropologist 77: 267-289.

Yacine, T. (1987) Poésie Berbère et Identité: Qasi Udefella, héraut des At Sidi Braham, Paris, Editions de la Maison des Sciences de l'Homme.

Yoffee, N. and G. L. Cowgill (eds.) (1988) The Collapse of Ancient States and Civilizations, Tucson, University of Arizona Press.

Zeltner, J. Cl. (1977) Les Arabes dans la Région du lac Tchad: Problèmes d'Origine et de Chronologie, Sarh (Chad), Centre d'études linguistiques.

_ (1980) Pages d'histoire du Kanem: pays tchadien, Paris, L'Harmattan.

_ (1988) Le Pays Tchadien dans la tourmente, 1880-1903, Paris, l'Harmattan.

Zézé Beke, P. (1989) Les Nyabwa et leurs généalogies, in Sources orales de l'histoire de l'Afrique, edited by Cl. H. Perrot, G. Gonnin and F. Nahimana, Paris, CNRS, pp. 127-147.

Tables

Table 1 Frequency distribution of words per section

Sequences	I		II		III		IV	
	Reign	Freq;	Reign	Freq.	Reign	Freq.	Reign	Freq.
	0	172	11	37	26	47	48	64
	1	34	Tr	28	27	76	49	44
	2	24	12	40	28	38	50	70
	3	36	13	204	29	41	51	41
	4	31	14	164	30	40	52	48
	5	19	15	113	31	79	53	38
	6	31	16	90	32	31	54	56
	7	43	17	111	33	34	55	63
	8	44	18	43	34	48	56	30
	9	65	19	53	35	44	57	39
	10	101	20	115	36	34	58	42
			21	104	37	74	59	36
			22	41	38	65	60	47
			23	37	39	46	61	37
			24	34	40	30	62	34
			25	44	41	31	63	36
					42	33	64	58
					43	32	65	38
					44	40	66/7	23
					45	51		
					46	71		
					47	36		

Table 2 Pattern of distribution of the frequency of words per sequence.

Sequence	I (1-10)	II (11-25)	III(26-47)	IV (48-66/7)	Total
No. of kings	10	15	22	19	67
n	428	1220	1021	844	3723
Minimum	19	34	31	23	19
Maximun	101	204	79	70	204
Range	82	170	48	47	185
Mean	42.80	81.33	46.40	44.42	45.74
Standard deviation	22.81	49.73	15.68	12.18	34.86
Coefficient of variation	0.53	0.61	0.33	0.27	0.63

Table 3 Syntactic structures of the Diwan

Sequence I	Sequence II	Sequence III	Sequence IV
1 F4-11 F3-1 F5	11 F1-20 F3-1 F5	26- F1-10 F2 F3-12 F5	48 F1-4 F2 F3-31 F4-1 F5
2 F1-11 F5	12 F1-17 F3-1 F5	27- F1-26 F2 F3-12 F5	49 F1-4 F2 F3-21 F5
3 F1-15 F2 F3-1 F5	13 F1-191 F5	28 F1-4 F2 F3-9 F5	50 F1-3 F2 F3-43 F4-1 F5
4 F1-10 F3-5 F5	14 F1-157 F3-3 F5	29 F1-7 F2 F3-9 F5	51 F1-4 F2-17 F4-1 F5
5 F1-8 F5	15 F1-85 F3-7 F5	30 F1-6 F2 F3-9 F5	52 F1-4 F2 F3-21 F4-1 F5
6 F1-11 F3-1 F5-4	16 F1-68 F3-1 F5	31 F1-3 F2 F3-1 F5	53 F1-5 F2 F3-9 F4-1 F5
7 F1-21 F2 F3-2 F5	17 F1-16 F2-63 F3-5 F5	32 F1-1 F2 F3-5 F5	54 F1-4 F2 F3-31 F4-1 F5
8 F1-20 F2 F3-1 F5	18 F1-16 F3-5 F5	33 F1-4 F2 F3-5 F5	55 F1-16 F4-1 F5-12 F3-12
9 F1-20 F2-24 F3-1 F5	19 F1-51 F3-1 F5	34 F1-3 F2-17 F3-2 F5	56 F1-11 F4-1 F5
10 F1-9 F2-65 F3-1 F5	20 F1-24 F3-72 F5	35 F1-5 F2-16 F3-2 F5	57 F1-6 F2-9 F4-1 F5
	21 F1-32 F3-49 F5	36 F1-4 F2 F3-4 F5	58 F1-5 F2-8 F3-5 F4-1 F5
	22 F1-9 F2 F3-7 F5	37 F1-4 F2-43 F3-1 F5	59 F1-4 F2 F3-8 F4-1 F5
	23 F1-7 F2 F3-7 F5	38 F1-4 F2-22 F3-12 F5	60 F1-6 F2-20 F4-1 F5
	24 F1-2 F2 F3-7 F5	39 F1-4 F2-15 F3-1 F4 F5	61 F1-4 F2 F3-8 F4-1 F5
	25 F1-12 F2 F3-8 F5	40 F1-4 F2 F3-1 F5	62 F1-3 F2 F3-4 F4-1 F5
		41 F1-4 F2 F3-3	63 F1-19 F4-1 F5
		42 F1-7 F2 F3-1 F5	64 F1-26 F3-12 F4-1 F5
		43 F1-4 F2-9 F3-3	65 F1-4 F3-14 F4-1 F5
		44 F1-3 F2 F3-13 F5	66 F1-19
		45 F1-4 F2-20 F3-1 F5	
		46 F1-5 F2-41 F3-1 F5	
		47 F1-3 F2-7 F3-1	

Key:
F1= Then came...
F2= He also lived.
F3= When his end arrived, he died at...
F4= At his time...
F5= His reign lasted for (x) years.

Table 4 Frequency distribution of formulas in the Diwan

Formula	F1	F2	F3	F4	F5	Total
Sequence I	11	5	9	–	11	36
Sequence II	15	6	14	–	15	50
Sequence III	23	23	23	1	21	91
Sequence IV	17	11	11	16	15	70
Total	67	45	57	17	62	248

Key:
F1= Then comes...
F2= He also lived.
F3= When his end arrived, he died at..
F4= At his time...
F5= His reign lasted for (x) years.

Table 5 Frequency distribution of sets of information blocks

Number of combined sets	1	2	3	4	5	Total
Sequence I	_	2	4	5	_	11
Sequence II	_	1	8	6	_	15
Sequence III	_	_	2	19	2	23
Sequence IV	1	_	2	6	8	17
Total	1	3	16	36	10	67

Table 6 Pattern of succession of information block sets

Variants	Frequency	1	2	3	4	5
Sequence I						
1	2		FI-F5 (2,5)			
2	4			FI-F3-F5 (1,4,6,11)		
3	5				F1-F2-F3-F5 (3,7,8,9,10)	
Sequence II						
1	1		F1-F5 (13)			
2	8			FI-F3-F5 (12,14-16, 18-21)		
3	6				F1-F2-F3-F5 (17, 22-26)	
Sequence III						
1	2		F1-F2-F3 (41,43)			
2	20				F1-F2-F3-F5 (27-38,40, 42, 44-47, 49)	
3	2				F1-F2-F3-F4-F5 (39, 48)	
Sequence IV						
1	1	FI (66)				
2	2			F1-F4-F5 (56, 63)		
3	3			F1-F2-F4-F5 (51,57,60)		
4	1			F1-F4-F5-F3 (55)		
5	2				F1-F3-F4-F5 (64,65)	
6	8				F1-F2-F3-F4-F5 (50,52-54,58,59 61,62)	

Key:
FI= Then comes...
F2= He also lived.
F3= When his end arrived, he died at...
F4= At his time...
F5= His reign lasted for (x) years.

Table 7 Lengths of reigns in the Diwan

Sequence	I		II		III		IV	
	Reign	Length	Reign	Length	Reign	Length	Reign	Length
	1	20	11	4	26	5	48	33
	2	16	12	12	27	10	49	23
	3	250	13	55	28	4	50	19
	4	60	14	27	29	2	51	1
	5	50	15	17	30	0.9	52	19
	6	250/300	16	28	31	5	53	7
	7	20	17	40	32	1	54	53
	8	16	18	29	33	1	55	16.7
	9	44	19	20	34	33	56	7.7
	10	4	20	20	35	0.9	57	19.9
			21	20	36	2	58	40
			22	4	37	8	59	19
			23	1	38	8	60	14
			24	1	39	1	61	16
			25	1	40	4	62	2.7
					41	0.5	63	46
					42	1	64	17
					43	-	65	8
					44	5	66/7	-
					45	5		
					46	1		
					47	5		

Table 8 Pattern of distribution of reigns' lengths throughout the sequences

Sequence	I	II	III	IV	Total
Reigns	**1-10**	**11-25**	**26-47**	**48-66/7**	**67**
N	730/780	279	123.3	340	1472.3/1522.3
Minimum	4	1	0	0	0
Maximum	250/300	55	33	53	250/300
Range	246/296	54	33	53	250/300
Mean	73/78	18.60	5.60	17.89	21.16/23.06
Standard deviation	90.04/100.51	15.18	7.97	14.44	39.02/47.28
Coefficient of variation	1.23/1.28	0.81	1.42	0.80	1.84/2.05

Table 9 Distribution of classes of reigns' lengths

Sequence	I	II	III	IV	Total
Reigns	1-10	11-25	26-47	48-66/7	67
1 (0-0.9 year)	_	_	4	2	6
2 (1-8 years)	1	5	15	5	26
3 (10-19.9 years)	2	2	1	8	13
4 (20-29 years)	2	6	1	1	10
5 (30-39 years)	_	_	1	1	2
6 (40-49 years)	1	1	_	2	4
7 (50-60 years)	2	1	_	1	4
8 (250-300 years)	2	_	_	_	2

Table 10 Pattern of numbers selected for reigns' lengths

Class	1	2	3	4	5	6	7	8
	–	1(9)	10(1)	20(5)	–	40(3)	50(1)	250(2)
	–	2(2)	12(1)	–	–	–	–	–
	–	2.7(1)	–	–	–	–	–	–
	–	–	–	23(1)	33(2)	–	53(1)	–
	–	4(5)	14(1)	–	–	44(1)	–	–
	0.5(1)	5(4)	–	25(1)	–	–	55(1)	–
	–	–	16(3)	–	–	–	–	– .
	–	–	16.7(1)	–	–	–	–	–
	–	7(1)	17(2)	27(1)	–	–	–	–
	–	7.7(1)	–	–	–	–	–	–
	–	8(3)	–	28(1)	–	–	–	–
	0.9(2)	–	19(3)	29(1)	–	–	–	–
	–	–	19.9(1)	–	–	–	–	–
	–	–	–	–	–	–	60(1)	300(1)
Total	3	26	13	10	2	4	4	3

(1) = the frequency recorded in the Diwan.

Table 11 List of numbers recorded in the Diwan

Sequence	I	II	III	IV
	1 20	11 4	26 25	48 33
	2 16	12 12	27 10	49 23
	3 250	13 2, 55, 300	28 4	50 19
	4 60	100,000, 120,000	29 2	51 1
	5 50	14 1, 27	30 9	52 19
	6 250, 300	15 17, 100, 200	31 5	53 7, 7
	7 20	16 28	32 1	54 53
	8 16	17 1, 40, 41,000	33 1	55 16, 7
	9 44, 300, 300, 300	18 29	34 33	56 7, 7
	10 7, 4	19 2, 20	35 9	57 19, 9
		20 20	36 2	58 40
		21 1, 4, 20	37 8	59 7, 19
		22 4	38 8	60 14
		23 1	39 1	61 2, 16
		24 1	40 4	62 2, 7˙
		25 1	41 5	63 46
			42 1	64 17
			43 -	65 8
			44 5	66/7 -
			45 5	
			46 1, 1	
			47 5	

Table 12 The Kotoko numerological system compared to that inferred from the Diwan

Class

1 1-9

K	_	1	2	3	4	5	6	7	8	9
D	_	1	2	2.7	4	5	_	7	7.7	9

2 10-19

K	10	11	12	13	14	15	16			
D	10	_	12	_	14	_	16	16.7	17	19 19.9

3 20-29

K	_	_	22	_	24	25	26			
D	_	_	_	23	_	25	_	27	28	29

4 30-39

K	30	_	_	_	_	_	36	_	38
D	_	_	_	33	_	_	_	_	_

5 40-49

K	40	_	_	_	_	_	_	_	_	49
D	40	_	_	_	44	_	_	_	_	_

6 50-59

K	_	_	_	_	_	_	56
D	50	_	_	53	_	55	_

7 60-69

K	60	_	62
D	60	_	_

8 > 100

K	100	112	180	196	313	500	1000-1	1000	
D	100			200	250	300	41,000	100,000	120,000

(The Kotoko numerological system is adapted from Lebeuf 1976)
K= Kotoko
D= Diwan

able 13 List of toponyms recorded in the Diwan

equence I	II	III	IV
Shimi	11 Ghamazurida	26 Djimi, Dammasak	48 Ghasrakmu
–	12 E gypt	27 M.l.f.la	49 Djimi
Y.ri Ar.f.sa	13 Mekka, Egypt	28 Djimi	50 Lada, Ghasrakmu
M.lan, Kanem	14 Ghamtilu, B.li Gh.na	29 Djimi	51 Zamtam
–	15 Khayr.K.r.s.mu, F.f.s	30 S.f.yari Gh.r.r.na	52 Ghasrakmu
Kuluwan	16 Dj.dj.s.ka, Gh.z.runa	31 Khaga, Kanem	53 Kitali
T.t.nuri B.r.rya	17 Zamtan	D.magh.ya	54 Alaw
D.r.q Magh.djabadmi	18 D.r.ya Gh.y.mutu	32 Dakakiya	55 D.kana
Kawar,D.r.ka,	19 Shima, Malli	33 Ghuduru	56 Ghasrakmu
S.k.d.m, Zaylan	20 Zuzu, Diskama	34 B.gh.r.mi K.n.ntu	57 Ghasrakmu
) Ghanatkamana	21 Baghirmi, Djimi	35 Afnu Kunu	58 Ghasrakmu
	22 Yus.b	36 Nanigham	59 Ghasrakmu
	23 Ghaliwa	37 F.m.l.fa	60 Ghasrakmu
	24 Ghaliwa	38 Zamtan	61 Ghasrakmu
	25 Nanigham	39 Am.za	62 Ghasrakmu
		40 Aghaquwa	63 Ghasrakmu
		41 Maza	64 Ghasrakmu
		42 T.r.m.ta	65 Ghala
		43 Maghdjib.d N.ri Karburi	66 –
		44 Matakla GH.m.r.	
		45 M.k.da	
		46 Gh.m.t.l.r.ka	
		47 B.r.b.di	

Table 14 Frequency distribution of toponyms according to categories

Sequence	I	II	III	IV	Total
Land	1	4	1	–	6
Residence	5	1	1	1	8
Important localities	–	3	–	–	3
Death places	8	14	23	17	62

Table 15 Pattern of distribution of toponyms

Sequence	I	II	III	IV	Total
None	2	_	_	2	4
Single	8	12	19	7	46
Pair	_	2	_		2
Triplet	_	_	1	_	1
Multiple (x12)	_	_	_	1	1

Table 16 Frequency distribution of toponyms

Sequence	I	II	III	IV	Total
None	2	–	–	2	4
1	5	11	20	17	53
2	2	2	1	1	6
3	–	2	1	–	3
5	1	–	–	–	1

Table 17 List of ethnonyms recorded in the Diwan

Sequence I		II		III		IV	
1	–	11	Gh.m.z.m	26	–	48	–
2	–	12	Kay	27	Bulala	49	Bulala
3	Kay	13	Tubu, Banu Hummay Egyptians	28	Bulala	50	–
4	–	14	Kay	29	Bulala		
5	–	15	Tubu	30	Bulala		
6	–	16	Dabir, Bedouin Arabs	31	Bulala		
7	Banu Gh.l.gh Habasha	17	M.gh.r.ma	32	Bulala		
8	Banu Kay	18	M.gh.r.ma	33	Bulala		
9	Tamaghar	19	Fellata	34	–		
10	Tamaghar	20	Kankuna				
		21	–				
		22	Saw				
		23	Saw				
		24	Saw				
		25	Saw				

Table 18 Frequency distribution of patronyms

Sequence	I		II		III		IV	
	1	1	11	4	26	4	48	4
	2	4	12	4	27	6	49	2
	3	4	13	4	28	2	50	6
	4	2	14	4	29	3	51	2
	5	3	15	10	30	2	52	3
	6	2	16	6	31	4	53	2
	7	5	17	6	32	1	54	3
	8	4	18	4	33	2	55	2
	9	4	19	4	34	4	56	1
	10	6	20	9	35	5	57	2
			21	5	36	2	58	2
			22	3	37	8	59	2
			23	2	38	3	60	2
			24	1	39	4	61	2
			25	3	40	2	62	1
					41	2	63	2
					42	3	64	2
					43	2	65	2
					44	4	66/7	2
					45	4		
					46	6		
					47	2		

Table 19 Descriptive statistics on the distribution of patronyms

Sequence	I	II	III	IV	Global
N	35	69	72	44	220
Minimum	1	1	1	1	1
Maximum	6	10	8	6	10
Range	5 9	7	5	9	
Mean	3.5	4.6	3.42	2.3	3.38
Standard deviation	1.43	2.3	1.7	1.05	1.87
Coefficient of variation	0.40	0.50	0.49	0.45	0.55

Table 20 Distribution of single patronyms

Sequence I	II	III	IV
2 K.r.m	11 Ladsu, Ab.li, B.q.ru	26 Hafsa, Amiya	50 L.fiya
3 Ghafalu, H.ra	12 T.k.r.m, Gh.m.z.	29 F.mafa	54 Ghargur.
5 Fukalshi	13 Kitna, B.r.ma	30 Abu Bakr Liyatu	57 F.sham
7 Tumayu, Makamsi	15 F.d.l.	32 Said	60 Hamdun
8 Ghat.djaya, Zakna	16 Abd el-Rahman	34 D.l.t.	
9 Ar.s.na, Sanᶜana	17 Dabali, L.f.r.d	35 Nikali	
10 T.f.su, Ar.kay.wann	18 M.t.la, Yun.s	41 Matala	
	19 L.k.m.ma	42 Amr	
	20 Kakudi, Saᶦᶜiduma	44 Ghadji, Imata	
	Ghadi, D.r.gh.z.na		
	25 K.gh.la, W.r.ma		

Table 21 Frequency distribution of the selected patronyms

Patronym	I	II	III	IV	Total
Duku	2				2
Funa	2				2
Katur	2				2
Ayuma	2				2
Bulu	2				2
Arku	2				2
Hummay		2			2
F.sama		2			2
S.karam		2			2
Ghayu		2			2
Nasi			2		2
Ahmad				2	2
Arsu	3				3
Sayf	2	1			3
Bakuru		3			3
Batku		3			3
Fatima		2	1		3
Aisha	1		1	1	3
Hawa	3	1			4
Salmama		4			4
Dawud			4		4
Zaynab		2		2	4
Abd alDjalil		3	1	2	6
Bir		4	3		7
Umar			5	2	7
Kaday			6	2	8
Ali			1	8	9
Ibrahim	2	1	5	2	10
Abd Allah		5	4	1	10
Idris			6	4	10
Uthman			9	1	10

Dunama	5	4	8	17
Muhammad	2	10	5	17

Table 22 Diversity of patronyms

Sequence	I	II	III	IV
Arab	4	11	19	12
Local	19	27	6	5
Female	8	10	8	2
Male	15	28	18	15
Total	23	38	26	17

Table 23 Distribution of Arab and local patronyms according to gender

Sequence	I	II	III	IV	Total
Frequency					
Arab names	6	24	55	30	115
Female	4	4	5	3	16
Male	2	20	50	27	99
Local names	27	40	16	14	95
Female	6	9	3	1	18
Male	21	31	13	13	77
Total	33	64	71	44	210
Ratios					
Arab/local	0.28	0.60	3.43	2.14	1.21
Female/male	0.47	0.21	0.12	0.10	0.19
AF/LF	0.66	0.44	1.66	3.00	0.88
AM/LM	0.09	0.64	3.84	2.07	1.28
Arab F/M	2.00	0.20	0.10	0.11	0.16
Local F/M	0.28	0.29	0.23	0.07	0.23

Key: A = Arab; F = Female; L = Local; M = Male

Table 24 List of kings' patronyms

Reign	Local names	Mixed names	Arab names
Sequence I			
1			Sayf
2			Ibrahim
3	Duku		
4	Funa		
5	Arsu		
6	Katur		
7	Ayuma		
8	Bulu		
9	Arku		
10			Hawa
Sequence II			
11			Abd al-Djali
12	Hummay		
13	Dunama		
14	Bir		
15		Abd Allah Bakuru	
16	Salmama		
17	Dunama		
18	Kaday		
19	Bir		
20			Ibrahim
21			Abd Allah
22	Salmama		
23	Kuri Junior		
24	Kuri Senior		
25			Muhammad
Sequence III			
26			Idris

27			Dawud
28			Uthman
29			Uthman
30		Abu Bakr Liyatu	
31			Umar
32			Said
33	Kaday Afnu		
34	Bir		
35		Uthman K.l.n.ma	
36	Dunama		
37			Abd Allah
38			Ibrahim
39	Kaday		
40	Dunama		
41			Muhammad
42			Amr
43			Muhammad
44	Ghadji		
45			Uthman
46			Umar
47			Muhammad

Sequence IV

48			Ali
49			Idris
50			Muhammad
51			Ali
52	Dunama		
53			Abd Allah
54			Idris
55			Muhammad
56			Ibrahim
57			Al Hadj Umar
58			Ali
59	Dunama		

60		Al Hadj Hamdun	
61			Muhammad
62	Dunama Junior		
63			Ali
64			Ahmad
65	Dunama		
66			Ibrahim
67			Ali

Table 25 Diversity of kings' patronyms

Sequence	I	II	III	IV	Total
No of kings	10	15	22	20	67
Arab patronyms	3	5	10	7	15
Local patronyms	7	5	4	2	14
Mixed patronyms	–	1	2	–	3
Total	10	11	16	9°	32
Ratio Arab/local	0.42	1.00	2.50	3.50	1.07

Table 26 Frequency distribution of kings' patronyms

Rank	Patronym	I	II	III	IV	Frequency
1	Dunama		2	2	4	8
2	Muhammad		1	3	3	7
3	Ibrahim	1	1	1	2	5
	Ali				5	5
4	Abd Allah		1	1	1	3
	Bir		2	1		3
	Kaday		1	2		3
	Umar			2	1	3
	Idris			1	2	3
5	Kuri		2			2
	Salmama		2			2
6	Single	Sayf	Abd al	Dawud	Al Hadj	
		Duku	Djalil	Abu Bakr	Hamdun	
		Funa		Liyatu		
		Arsu	Hummay			
		Katur		Said	Ahmad	
		Ayuma	Abd Allah	Uthman		
		Bulu	Bakuru	K.l.n.ma		
		Arku				
		Hawa		Amr		
				Ghadji		

Table 27 Patterns of kinship, affinity and rivalry

Sultan Father	Mother	Mother's	Rival father	
Sequence I				
1 Sayf	Al Sahh	Princess Baghdad	King of	–
2 Ibrahim	Sayf	Aisha	K.r.m	–
3 Duku	Ibrahim	Ghafalu	H.r.a	–
4 Funa	Duku	– –	–	
5 Arsu	Funa	Fukalshi	–	–
6 Katur	Arsu	– –	–	
7 Ayuma	Katur	Tumayu	Makamsi	–
8 Bulu	Ayuma	Ghat.djaya	Zakna	–
9 Arku	Bulu	Ar.s.na	San^cana	–
10 Hawa	Arku	T.f.su	Ar.kay.wann	–
Sequence II				
11 Abd al-Djalil	Ladsu	Ab.li	B.q.ru	–
12 Hummay	Abd al-Djalil	T.k.r.m	Gh.m.z	–
13 Dunama	Hummay	Kitna	B.r.ma	–
14 Bir	Dunama	F.sama	S.karam	–
15 Abd Allah Bakuru	Bir	Zaynab	F.d.l	–
16 Salmama	–	Hawa	Abd al-Rahman	–
17 Dunama	Salmama	Dabali	Batku	Ghayu
18 Kaday	–	M.t.la	Yun.s	Dunama
19 Bir	Dunama	Zaynab	L.k.m.ma	–
20 Ibrahim	Bir	Kakudi	Sa^ciduma	Muhammad
21 ABd Allah	Kaday	Fatima	--	Ghayu
22 Salmama	Abd Allah	K.ma	–	–
23 Kuri the Younger	Abd Allah	–	–	–
24 Kuri the Elder	Abd Allah	–	–	–
25 Muhammad	Abd Allah	W.r.ma	–	–
Sequence III				
26 Idris	Ibrahim	Hafsa	Nasi	–

27 Dawud	Ibrahim	Fatima	Nasi	Abd al Djalil
28 Uthman	Dawud	–	–	–
29 Uthman	Idris	F;Mafa	–	–
30 Abu Bakr Liyatu	Dawud	–	–	–
31 Umar	Idris	–	–	--
32 Said	–	–	–	–
33 Kaday Afnu	Idris	–	–	–
34 Bir	Idris	–	–	Muhammad
35 Uthman K.l.n.ma	Dawud	– Ka'aku	– Kaday	Nikali
36 Dunama	Umar	–	–	–
37 Abd Allah	Umar	–	– D.gh.l.ma Ibrahim	Abd Allah
38 Ibrahim	Uthman	–	–	Kaday
39 Kaday	Uthman	– –	Dunama	
40 Dunama	Bir	–	–	–
41 Muhammad	–	Matala	–	–
42 Amr	–	Aisha	–	–
43 Muhammad	Kaday	–	–	–
44 Ghadji	–	Imata	–	Muhammad
45 Uthman	Kaday	–	–	Ali
46 Umar	Abd Allah	–	–	Muhammad
47 Muhammad	Muhammad	–	–	–

Sequence IV

48 Ali	Dunama	–	–	Kaday
49 Idris	–	Aisha	–	–
50 Muhammad	Idris	Zaynab	–	Kaday
51 Ali	Idris	Zaynab	–	–
52 Dunama	Muhammad	–	–	Abd al Djalil
53 Abd Allah	Dunama	–	–	–
54 Idris	Ali	–	–	Abd al Djalil
55 Muhammad	Idris	–	–	–
56 Ibrahim	–	–	–	–

57 Al Hadj Umar	F.s.ham	_	_	_
58 Ali	Al Hadj Umar	_	_	_
59 Dunama	Ali	_	_	_
60 Al Hadj Hamdun	Dunama	_	_	_
61 Muhammad	Al Hadj Hamdun	_	_	_
62 Dunama the Younger	_	_	_	_
63 Ali	Al Hadj Dunama	_	_	_
64 Ahmad	Ali	_	_	_
65 Dunama	Ahmad	_	_	_
66 Ibrahim	_	_	_	_
67 Ali	Ibrahim	_	_	_

Table 28 Frequency distribution of titles

Titles	I	II	III	IV	Total
Arab	13	27	31	24	95
Khalife	1	–	–	–	1
Sultan	10	21	27	24	82
Shaykh	–	1	–	–	1
Prince	–	2	–	–	2
King (Malik)	2	3	2	–	7
Ulema	–	–	2	–	2
Local	–	3	6	2	11
ᶜan.d.k.ma	–	1	–	–	1
Kayghama	–	–	4	–	4
Kanema	–	–	1	–	1
Yerima	–	1	1	–	2
Ghumsa	–	1	–	2	3
None	2	1	1	–	4
Diversity	4	8	7	2	12

Table 29 Frequency distribution of events

Events	I	II	III	IV	Total
Peaceful					
Expansion	1	–	–	2	3
Etiquette	1	2	–	–	3
Pilgrimage	–	2	–	3	5
Gifts	–	1	–	–	1
Islam and learning	–	–	–	7	7
Harmful					
Sacrilege	–	1	–	–	1
Famine	–	–	–	6	6
Exodus	–	–	1	–	1
Conflictual					
Dispute	–	4	9	–	13
Death sentence	–	5	–	–	5
Murder	–	1	–	1	2
Parricide	–	1	–	–	1
Regicide	–	1	2	–	3
Sultan slain	–	4	8	–	12
Wars					
Intra-dynastic	–	1	4	2	7
Civil war	–	1	8	2	11
Foreign war	–	5	7	2	14
Diversity of events	2	12	6	8	17

Table 30 List of early Arab authors consulted

N° Author	Date	Residence	Country	Occupation
1 Al Khuwarizmi	846-7	Lower Oxus River	Mesopotamia	Clerk/geographer
2 Ibn Abd al Hakam	803-71	Cairo	Egypt	Scholar
3 Ibn Qutayba	889	Baghdad	Iraq	Scholar
4 Ibn Khurradadhbih	885	Baghdad	Iraq	High official
5 Al Yaqubi	897	Khurasan/Cairo	Iraq/Egypt	Clerk/traveller
6 Al Masudi	947	Cairo	Egypt	Scholar
- 'Akbar al Zaman' *	1000?	_	_	_
7 Ishaq b. al Husayn	950?	?	?	?
8 Ibn Hawqual	988	Cairo	Egypt	Geographer/Traveller
9 Al Burini	973-1050	Ghazna	Iran	Scholar
10 Al Bakri	1064	Cordova	Spain	Scholar
11 Al Marwazi	1120	Merv	Turkmenistan	Physician
12 Al Zuhri	1137	?	?	Scholar
13 Al Idrissi	1154	?	Morocco	Geographer
-'Kitab al Istibsar'*	1191	_	_	_
14 Yaqut	1179-1229	Baghdad/Cairo	Iraq/Egypt	Scholar
15 Al Qazwini	1202-1283	Baghdad	Iraq	Scholar
16 Ibn Khallikan	1211-1282	Damascus	Syria	Scholar
17 Ibn Said	1214-1269	Tunis	Ifriqiya	Geographer
18 Abu l. Fida	1273-1331	Hamah	Syria	Emir, scholar
19 Al Dimashqi	1256-1327	Damascus	Syria	Scholar
20 Al Tijani	1306-8	Tunis	Ifriqiya	Official
21 Al Umari	1301-1349	Damascus/Cairo	Syria/Egypt	Clerk
22 Ibn Battuta	1304-1368	Marrakech	Morocco	Official/traveller
23 Ibn Khaldun	1332-1406	Tunis/Cairo	Ifriqiya/Egypt	Scholar/politician
25 Al Maqrisi	1364-1442	Cairo	Egypt	Scholar
26 Al Qalqashandi	1355-1418	Cairo	Egypt	Clerk/scholar
27 Ibn Majid	1489-90	?	Eastern Africa	Navigator

* Title of book, author unknown

Table 31 Names of land, peoples, ethnic groups and localities of the Central Sudan in early Arabic sources

Author	Zaghawa	Kanim	Barnu	Kawar	Djimi	Manan	Kagha
Al Khuwarizmi	1	–	–	–	–	–	–
Ibn al Hakam	–	–	–	6	–	–	–
Ibn Qutayba	1	–	–	–	–	–	–
Ibn Khurradadhbih	1	–	–	–	–	–	–
Al Yaqubi	4	3	–	2	–	–	–
Al Masudi	2	1	–	–	–	–	–
'Akbar al Zaman'	2	–	–	–	–	–	–
Ishaq b. al Husayn	1	–	–	–	–	–	–
Ibn Hawqual	1	–	–	–	–	–	–
Al Burini	1	–	–	–	–	–	–
Al Bakri	–	2	–	–	–	–	–
Al Marwazi	–	1	–	–	–	–	–
Al Zuhri	1	–	–	–	–	–	–
Al Idrssi	4	6	–	11	2	2	–
'Kitab al Istibsar'	–	1	–	–	–	–	–
Yaqut	10	3	–	4	–	–	–
Al Qazwini	–	–	–	3	–	–	–
Ibn Khallikan	–	2	–	–	–	–	–
Ibn Said	5	25	–	10	3	4	2
Abu l. Fida	4	7	–	–	1	1	1
Al Dimashqi	5	8	–	2	2	2	1
Al Tijani	–	2	–	–	–	–	–
Al Umari	–	3	2	–	1	–	2
Ibn Battuta	1	–	2	–	–	–	–
Ibn Khaldun	4	3	1	1	1	–	–
Al Maqrizi	1	11	1	–	–	–	–
Al Qalqashandi	–	–	11	–	1	–	3
Ibn Majid	–	2	–	–	–	–	–

Table 32 The meanings of the term Zaghawa in early Arabic sources

Author	Land	Town	Kingdom	People	Neighbours
Al Khuwarizmi	1	1	–	–	–
Ibn Qutayba	–	–	–	1	Habasha
Ibn Khurradadhbih	1	–	–	–	Habasha
Al Yaqubi	–	–	1	3	HBSH
Al Masudi	–	–	1	1	Kanim
'Akbar al Zaman'	–	–	1	1	Nuba
Ishaq b. al-Husayn	–	1	–	1	Nuba
Ibn Hawqual	1	–	–	1	Fezzan?
Al Burini	–	1	–	1	Zandj
Al Zuhri	–	–	–	1	Zandj
Al Idrissi	–	4	–	2	Kanim
Yaqut	1	1	1	5	Nuba
Ibn Said	–	1	–	4	Kanim
Abu l. Fida	1	–	–	3	Nuba
Al Dimashqi	1	–	–	3	Hubush
Ibn Battuta	–	–	–	1	–
Ibn Khaldun	–	–	–	4	Kanim
Al Maqrizi	–	–	–	1	Nuba, Kanim

Table 33 The meanings of the term 'Kanim' in early Arabic sources

Author	Land	Town	Kingdom	People	Neighbours
Al Yaqubi	1	–	1	1	HBSH
Al Masudi	–	–	–	1	Zaghawa
Al Bakri	1	–	–	1	–
Al marwazi	1	–	–	–	–
Al Idrissi	3	–	–	1	Zaghawa
'Kitab al Istibsar'	1	–	–	–	–
Ibn Khallikan	–	1	–	1	–
Yaqut	3	–	–	–	–
Ibn Said	8	–	8	5	Zaghawa
Abu l. Fida	5	–	2	–	–
Al Dimashqi	4	1	–	1	Habasha
Al Tijani	–	–	2	–	–
Al Umari	1	–	2	–	–
Ibn Khaldun	2	–	1	–	–
Al Maqrisi	3	–	5	3	Fezzan
Ibn Majid	2	–	–	–	–

Table 34 References to Bornu kingdom in early Arabic sources

Author	Land	Kingdom	Total
Al Umari	2	_	2
Ibn Battuta	1	1	2
Ibn Khaldun	_	1	1
Al Maqrizi	_	1	1
Al Qalqashandi	1	7	8

Table 35 Comparative chronology

Diwan (Reigns 20-31)	Ibn Battuta (1304-1368)	Al Qalqashandi (1355-1418)	Al Maqrizi (1364-1442)	Lange (1977)
20 Ibrahim (20 yrs)		Al Hadj Ibrahim	Al Hadj Ibrahim (1300)	1296
21 Abd Allah (20 yrs)				1315
22 Salmama (4 yrs)				1335
23 Kuri the Younger (1 y)				1339
24 Kuri the Elder (1 y)				1340
25 Muhammad (1 y)				1341
26 Idris (25 yrs)	King Idris (1352-3)	Al Hadj Idris	Al Hadj Idris	1342
27 Dawud (10 yrs)			Da'ud b. Ibrahin	1366
28 Uthman b. Dawud(4 yrs)		Amr b. Idris	Umar b. Idris	1376
29 Uthman b. Idris (2 yrs)		Uthman b. Idris (1391)	Uthman b. Idris (before 1397-8)	1379
30 Abu Bakr Liyatu (9 mths)				1381
31 Umar b. Idris (5 yrs)			1382	

Table 36 Archaeological sites tested and dated in eastern Kanem

Site	Situatiol (N lat./E.Long.)	Lab. N°	Date B.P.	Date AD/BC (x2 sigma range)	Depth (m)
Kebir Bosa	16° 07'/18° 42'	Gif 4193	1480+/-100	AD 270 - 670	0.15-0.20
		Gif 4202	2360+/-100	BC 610 - 210	0.20
Site 4	16° 04'/18° 28'	Gif 4199	1170+/-90	AD 600 - 960	0.10-0.15
		Gif 4198	1230+/-100	AD 520 - 920	0.35
		Gif 4194	1580+/-100	AD 170 - 570	0.80
		G.D. Paris.	1670+/-80	AD 120 - 440	1.25
		Gif 4135	1400+/-100	AD 350 - 750	2.20
Krimé	16° 01'/18° 27'	Gif 4196	670+/-100	AD 1080 - 1480	0.30
		Gif 4197	1410+/-100	AD 340 - 740	1.00
Bochianga	16°07'/18° 26'	G.D. Paris	935+/-80	AD 855 - 1175	0.10
		Gif 2611	1500+/-100	AD 250 - 650	0.80
		Gif 2612	1500+/-100	AD 250 - 650	1.35
Nemra III	16° 18'/18° 31'	Gif 2613	730+/-90	AD 1040 - 1400	0.10-0.30
Toungour-Salado	16° 18'/18° 27'	Gif 2896	1340+/-100	AD 410 - 810	0.30
Site 97	15° 46'/18° 35'	Gif 4200	1250+/-100	AD 500 - 900	0.20
Bahali I	16° 13'/18° 26'	?	630+/-90	AD 1140 - 1500	?
Bahali IV	16° 11'/18° 23'	Gif 4201	1540+/-90	AD 230 - 590	0.20

(Source: Treinen-Claustre 1978, 1982)

Table 37 Distribution of potsherds in the stratigraphic sequences of the excavated Yobe sites in Northern Bornu

Stratigraphy	Yau (Mound 3) (Shaft A)	Birni Ghazzargamo (Cutting I	Ajere
Surface	57	88	60
1	50	266	58
2	108	304	39
3	98	178	15
4	429	229	31
5	278	219	26
6	192	198	59
7	271	109	43
8	75	190	103
9	225	183	111
10	157	197	
11	127	111	
12	142	12	
13	302	22	
14	412		
15	–		
16	1020		
17	477		
18	67		
19	64		
20	133		
21	13		
Total	4697	2306	545

(Source: Connah 1981)

Table 38 Distribution of cultural material according to reconstructed occupation units

Occupation (spits)	Pottery	Utilized sherds	Grinding equipment	Iron items and slag	Others	Total
Yau: Mound 3, Shaft A						
I(20-21)	146	–	–	1	2	149
II(18-19)	131	3	–	2	1	137
III(15 17)	1497	36	2	13	10	1557
IV(13-14)	714	12	1	9	8	744
V(10-12)	426	17	–	2	12	457
VI(8-9)	300	14	–	5	9	328
VII(-7)	463	7	–	5	4	479
VIII(4-5)	707	11	3	55	10	786
IX(1-3)	256	1	–	6	1	264
Total	4640	101	5	98	57	4901
Birni Ghazzargamo: Cutting I						
I(10-13)	342	7	–	3	1	353
II(7-9)	482	6	–	7	8	503
III(4-6)	646	19	2	5	3	675
IV(1-3)	748	25	1	1	11	786
Total	2218	57	3	16	23	2317
Ajere						
I(8-9)	214	2	2	1	3	222
II(5-7)	128	2	–	–	17	147
III(3-4)	46	–	–	–	3	49
IV(1-2)	97	1	–	–	10	108
Total	485	5	2	1	33	526

(Compiled from Connah 1981)

Table 39 Archaeological sites tested and dated in the Yobe flood-plain (northern Bornu)

Site	Situation (N.lat./ E.long.)	Lab. No	Date BP (x2 sigma range)	Date BC/AD	Depth (m)
Yau	13° 33'/13° 15'	N 477	675+/-110	AD 1055 - 1495	0.80-1.20
		N 479	990+/-110	AD 740 - 1180	3.70-3.95
		N 478	1020+/-90	AD 750 - 1110	4.90-5.00
		N 478	1100+/-90	AD 780 - 1140	7.00-7.75
Birni Ghazzargamo	13° 00'/12° 18'	N 481	330+/-105	AD 1410 - 1830	1.40-2.65

(Sources: Connah 1971, 1981)

Table 40 Distribution of cultural material and relative chronology of the Yobe settlements

Yau: Mound 3			Ajere			Birnin Gazargamo			Date
O.U.	No	%	O.U.	No	%	O.U.	No	%	AD
I	149	3.04							780-1140
II	137	2.79							
III	1557	31.76							750-1110
IV	744	15.18							
V	457	9.32							740-1180
VI	328	6.69							
VII	479	9.77							
VIII	786	16.03	I	222	42.20				1055-1495
IX	264	5.38	II	147	27.94				
			III	49	9.31	I	353	15.23	1300
			IV	108	20.53	II	503	21.70	
						III	675	29.13	
						IV	786	33.92	1800
Total	4901			526			2317		

(O.U. = Occupation Unit)

(Data compiled from Connah 1971, 1981)

Table 41 Distribution of pottery according to decoration techniques and forms

| Occupation unit | DECORATION TECHNIQUES | | | FORMS AND SHAPES | | | |
	Sgraffito	Grooving and ridging	Roulettes impressions	Everted bowls	Everted necked pots	Cone necked vessels	Pot-lids
Yau Mound 3: Shaft A							
I	4	2	129	1	–	2	–
II	10	1	113	1	–	2	–
III	43	36	1323	22	–	21	–
IV	11	16	633	13	–	17	1
V	5	3	376	7	–	12	1
VI	4	7	513	10	–	15	–
VII	3	4	173	4	–	2	–
VIII	7	8	654	4	1	10	–
IX	1	11	213	11	–	9	3
Total	88	88	4127	73	1	90	5
Ajere							
I	2	1	200	–	–	9	–
II	–	–	121	–	–	6	–
III	–	–	43	–	–	3	–
IV	–	–	93	–	–	4	–
Total	2	1	457	–	–	22	–
Birni Ghazzargamo, Cutting I							
I	9	11	252	–	18	1	38
II	17	14	347	–	39	–	43
III	39	30	440	–	65	–	58
IV	115	16	490	–	69	–	33
Total	180	71	1529	–	191	1	172

(Data compiled from Connah 1981)

Table 42 Radiocarbon dates from palaeoecological samples

No	Station	Area	Lab N°	Date B.P.	Date AD (calibrated)
Low lake levels					
1	Chari Delta	Southern shore	Gif 3460	510+/-90	1395+/-100
2	Bol Tandal	Kanem shore	Gif 1029	460+/-95	1420+/-105
3	Bol Berim	Kanem shore	I 4270	430+/-95	1430+/-105
4	Nioum	Kanem	Gif 1235	390+/-90	1450+/-100
5	Kouka	Bahr el Ghazzal	Gif 3681	360+/-90	1460+/-100
6	Foga	Mangari	T. 399	350+/-110	1460+/-120 or 1500+/-120
7	Bosso	Yobe	Birm. 391	110+/-80	1790+/-90 or 1830+/-90
High lake levels					
8	Ngouri	Bahr el Ghazzal	Gif 3549	260+/-120	1615+/-130
9	Karagou	Mangari	T. 402	230+/-80	1635+/-90
10	Nedeley	Bahr el Ghazzal	Gif 1096	140+/-90	1670+/-100

(Data compiled from Maley 1973, 1981, 1989)

Figures

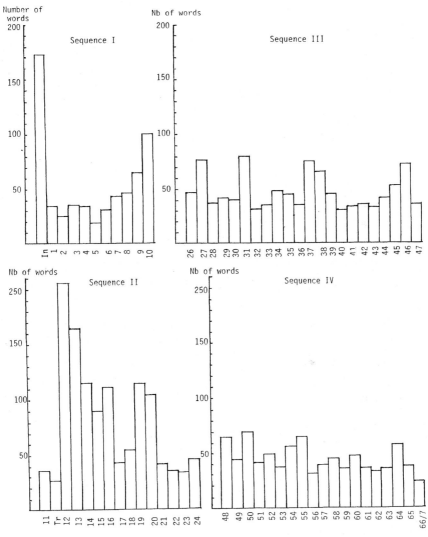

Key: In = Introduction; Tr = Transition

Figure 1 Fluctuations in the frequency distribution of words per section

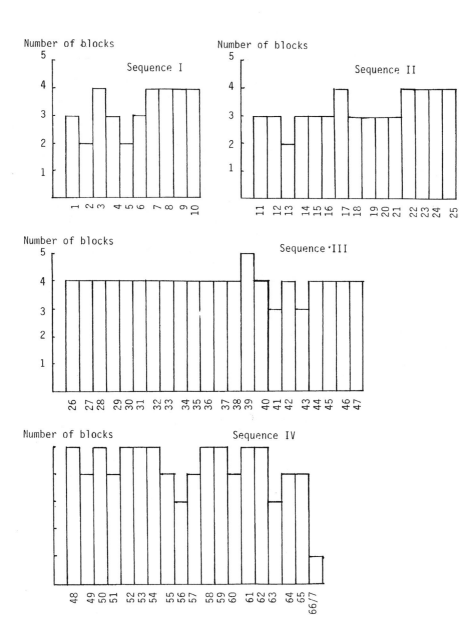

Figure 2 Fluctuations in the distribution of sets of information blocks

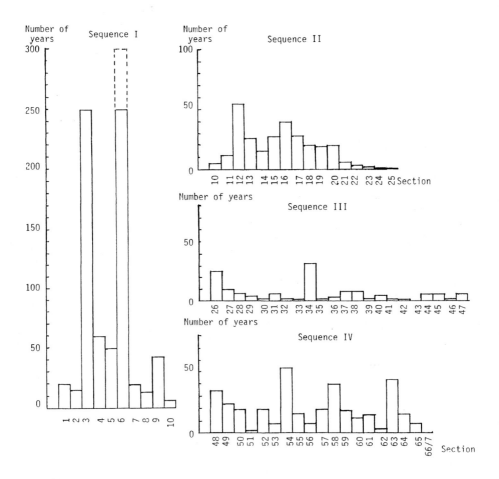

Figure 3 Fluctuations in the distribution of reigns' lengths

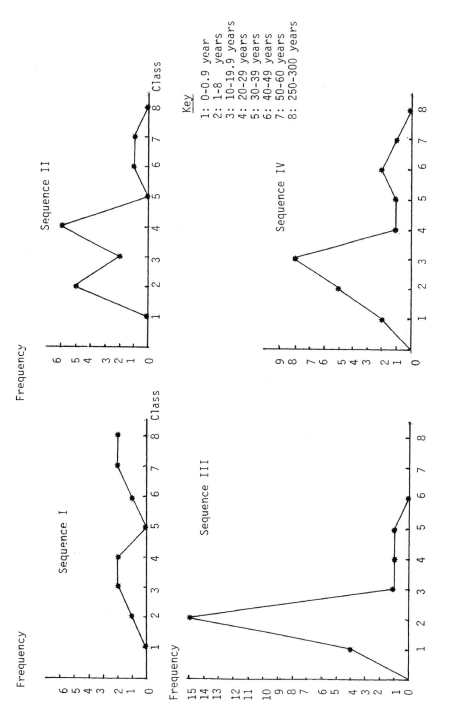

Figure 4 Distribution of reigns' lengths into classes of numbers

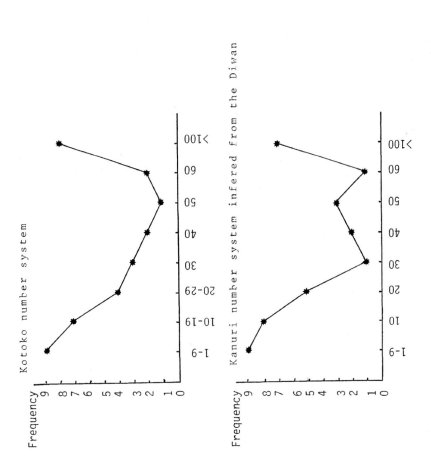

Figure 5 Comparison of the structures of Kotoko and Kanuri number systems

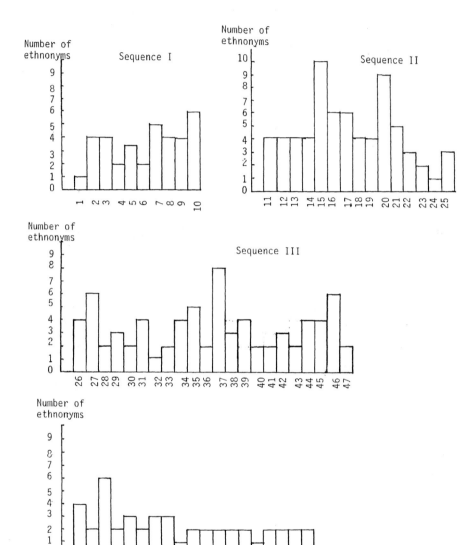

Figure 6 Fluctuations in the frequency distribution of ethnonyms

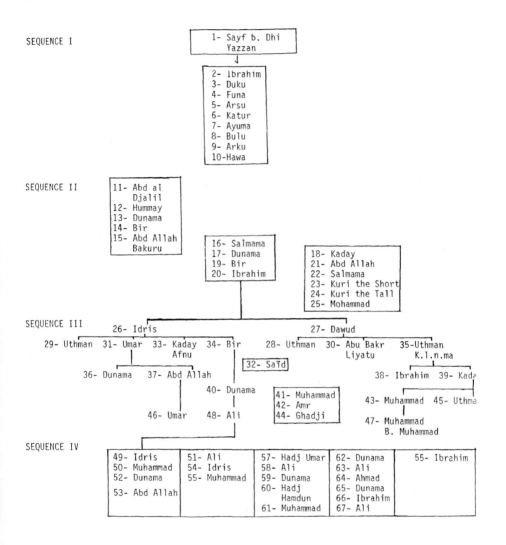

Figure 7 Patterns of succession to sultanship

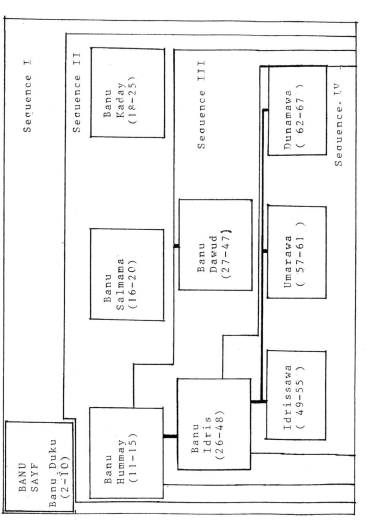

Figure 8 Lineages and 'descent groups' among the Sayfawa: genealogical patterns inferred from the Diwan

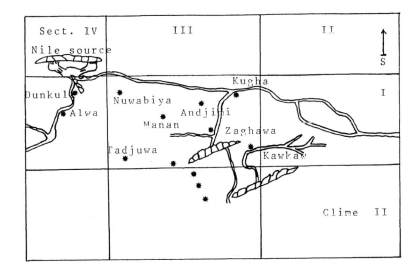

1 Map of eastern Central Sudan by Al Idrissi (1154)

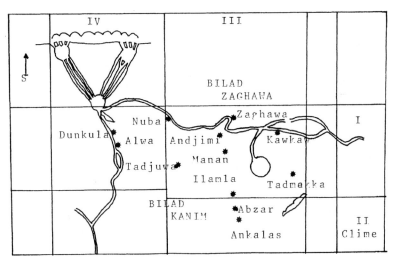

2 Map of eastern Central Sudan by Al Idrissi (1192)

Figure 9 Early maps of eastern and Central Sudan (1154 and 1192)

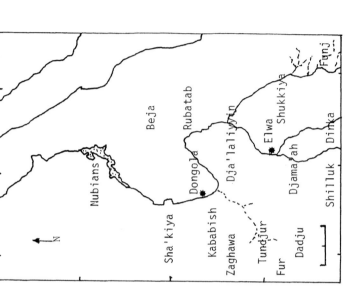

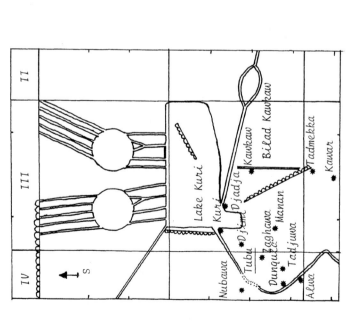

1 Ethnic groups and localities from the Central Sudan in the thirteenth century by Ibn Saïd (Source: Lange 1985: 267)

2 Distribution of ethnic groups in eastern Sudan from the twelfth to the sixteenth century (Source: Kropacek 1985: 435)

Figure 10 Distribution of ethnic groups and localities of Central and eastern Sudan during the first half of the second millennium AD (ethnic groups underlined)

Figure 11 Archaeological sites of the eastern Kanem and northern Bornu, and map of collected palaeoecological samples sites from the Lake Chad area .

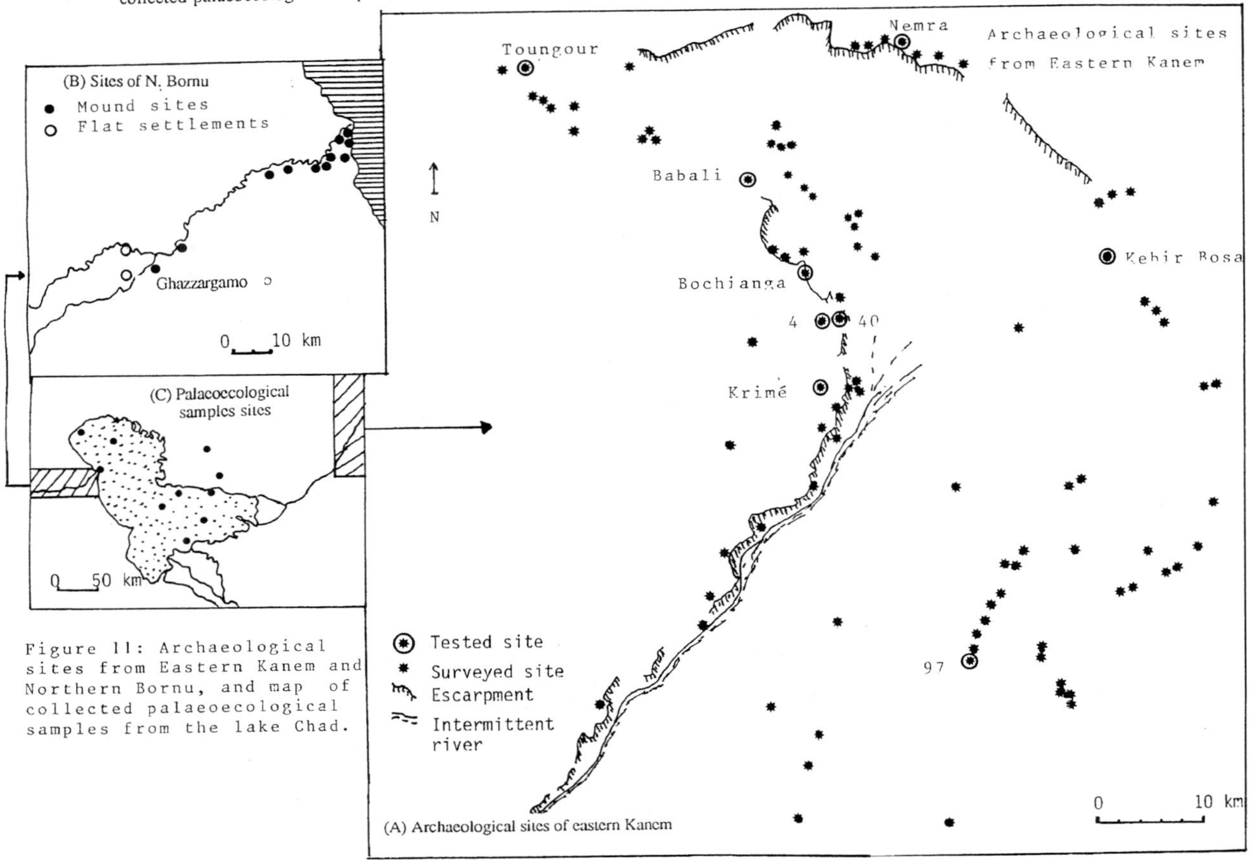

Figure 11: Archaeological sites from Eastern Kanem and Northern Bornu, and map of collected palaeoecological samples from the lake Chad.

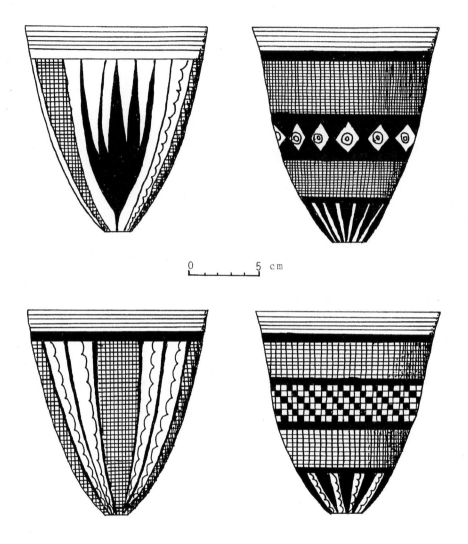

0 _____ 5 cm

Figure 12   Samples of the pottery from the 'Koro Toro Culture' (Source Treinen-Claustre 1982)

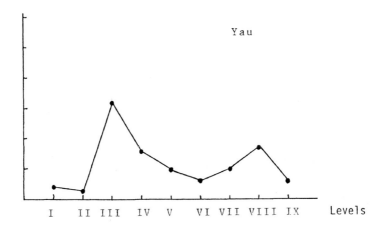

Yau

Levels

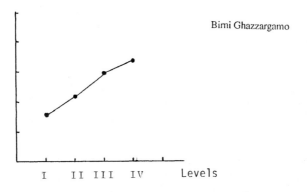

Birni Ghazzargamo

Levels

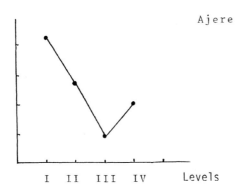

Ajere

Levels

Figure 13 Curves of the frequency distribution of archaeological material collected from the stratigraphic sequences of northern Bornu settlements.

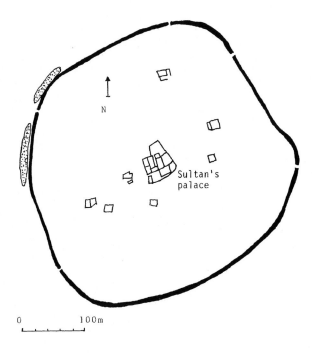

Figure 14   Map of Birnin Ghazzargamo, the capital city of the kingdom of Bornu (1450-1810) (redrawn with permission after Bivar and Shinnie, 1962, 'Old Kanuri caiptals', *Journal of African History* 3: 2; Cambridge University Press)

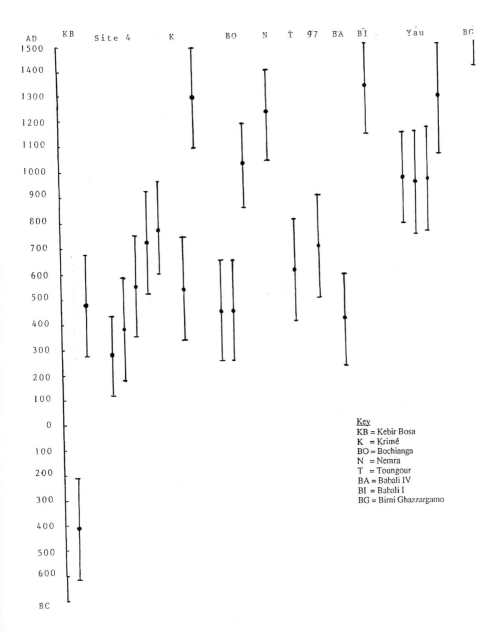

Figure 15 Radiocarbon chronology of archaeological sites from eastern Kanem and northern Bornu

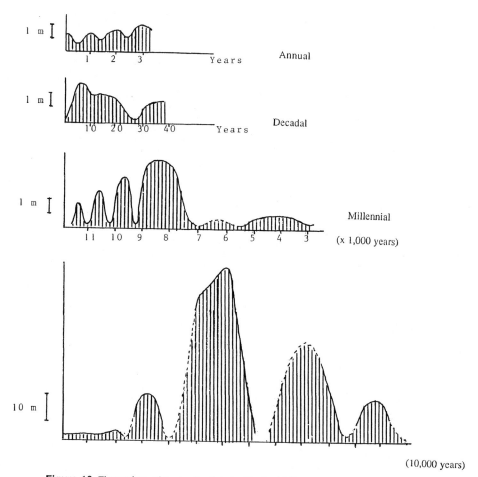

1 m   Years   Annual

1 m   Years   Decadal

1 m   Millennial

(x 1,000 years)

10 m

(10,000 years)

Figure 16 Fluctuations of the levels of Lake Chad at different and nested time-scales (with permission after Servant and Servant-Vildary 1980: 146)

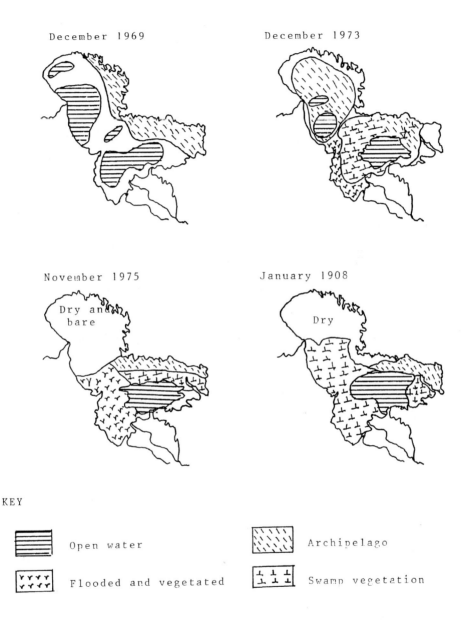

December 1969   December 1973

November 1975   January 1908

Dry and bare

Dry

KEY

Open water

Archipelago

Flooded and vegetated

Swamp vegetation

Figure 17 Variations in the distribution of water in Lake Chad (redrawn with permission from Grove 1985: 67)

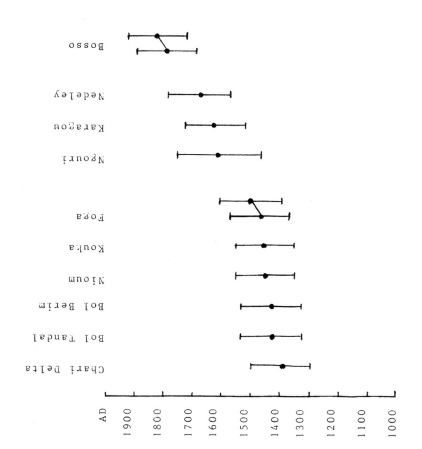

Figure 18 Radiocarbon chronology of the variations of Lake Chad levels during the last millennium (1000-1900) (data compiled from Maley 1981)

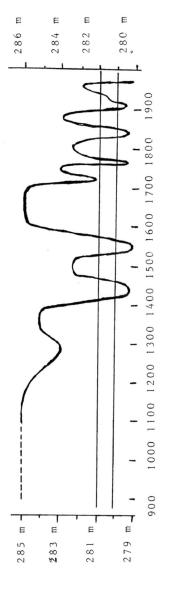

Figure 19 Curve of the fluctuations of Lake Chad levels during the last millennium
(1000-1900) (redrawn from Maley 1981: 58)

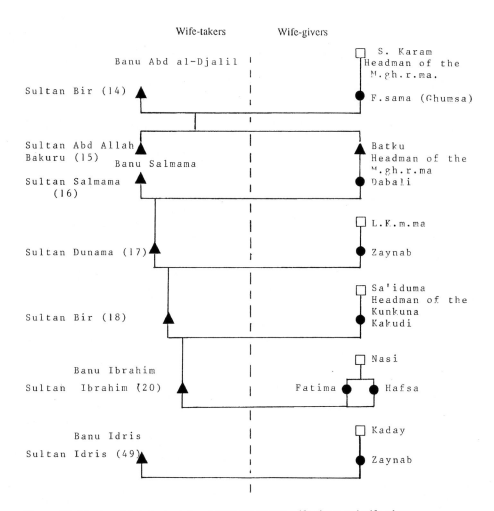

Figure 20 Matrimonial strategies inferred from the Diwan: wife-givers and wife-takers

Index

A

Abd al Djalil, 65, 66, 68, 71, 72, 73, 80, 93, 122
Abd Allah, 2, 6, 8, 9, 12, 14, 16, 51, 56, 59, 60, 61, 65, 72, 73, 74, 75, 76, 81, 82, 83, 90, 93, 94, 122, 124
Abd Allah al Saliliji, 90, 94
Abd Allah Bakuru, 6, 56, 59, 65, 72, 74, 81, 82, 122
Abd Allah D.gh.l.ma, 12, 75, 124
Abd el Kerim (H. Barth), 23, 24
Abd er Rahman, 23, 24, 25
Abd er-Rahman, 7
Abeche, 84
Abu al-Hadjdj, 2
Abu Bakr, 10, 70, 72, 73, 74
Abu Bakr Liyatu, 10, 70, 72, 74
Abu Ishaq Ibrahim, 90
Abu l. Fida, 91
Adam, 3
Adamawa, 22
Adams, W.Y., 129
Adrar-n-Ifogha, 106
Afnu, 11, 12, 59, 61, 62, 72, 74
Africa, 21, 22, 32, 36, 39, 49, 63, 96, 97, 105, 109, 115, 129, 131, 132, 133, 134, 135, 137, 138, 139, 140
African, 21, 28, 31, 32, 89, 97, 99, 105, 117, 128, 129, 130, 131, 133, 134, 135, 136, 137, 139, 140
Agari Galmami, 84
Aghaquwa, 13
Agid Burku, 22
Ahmad, 18, 22, 31, 33, 41, 55, 57, 61, 62, 72, 75, 93, 95, 107
Ahmad Furtu, 22, 33, 62, 95, 107
Ahmed bel Mejub, 26
Ahmed el Baghdadi, 22
Ahmedu ben Ahmedu, 22
Aïr, 106
Ajere, 111, 112, 113
Al Barnu, 94
Al Dimashqi, 91
Al Hadj Hamdun, 75
Al Hadj Ibrahim, 95

Al Hadj Umar, 75
Al Idrissi, 91
Al Kanim, 94
Al Khuwarizmi, 90
Al Masudi, 90
Al Mustancir, 38
Al Qalqashandi, 39, 90, 92, 94
Al Umari, 91, 94
Al Yaqubi, 90, 91
Al Zahir Barquq, 92
Al Zuhri, 90
Alage, 54
Alauma, 22, 39, 40, 52, 55, 57, 137
Alaw, 16, 62
Alexandre, 99, 129
Ali, 14, 15, 16, 17, 18, 31, 35, 52, 57, 60, 61, 71, 72, 73, 74, 75, 77, 81, 82, 93, 125
Ali Shawa, 17
Allei Ouarimi, 84
Almeria, 89
Alur, 100, 123, 124, 140
Alwa, 90, 92
Am.za, 13
Amir, 2, 3, 84
Amiya, 10, 70
Amr, 13, 70, 72, 73, 74, 77, 92, 94
Anni, 84
Arab, 22, 23, 26, 36, 39, 64, 70, 72, 73, 74, 75, 89, 92, 117
Arabic, 31, 32, 41, 43, 50, 68, 84, 89, 93, 128, 137
Arbaumont, 40, 75, 76, 84, 132
Ardea Bazeunmi, 84
Aremkar, 84
Arfakhshadh Makhshadh, 3
Arguin, 22
Arku, 4, 38, 56, 59, 65, 72, 82
Arkuma, 3
Arsu, 3, 4, 60, 72, 80
Asianti, 22
Asiatic, 134
Ayuma, 4, 64, 65, 72